CW01337592

A CHOICE OF
BROWNING'S VERSE

A Choice of

BROWNING'S
Verse

selected
with an introduction by
EDWARD LUCIE-SMITH

FABER AND FABER
3 Queen Square
London

First published in this edition in 1967
by Faber and Faber Limited
3 Queen Square London W.C.1
Reprinted 1974
Printed in Great Britain
by R. MacLehose and Company Limited
The University Press Glasgow
All rights reserved
© this selection Faber and Faber
1967

ISBN 0 571 08170 3 (Faber Paper Covered Editions)
ISBN 0 571 08105 3 (hard bound edition)

CONDITIONS OF SALE

This book is sold subject to the condition that it shall not, by way
of trade or otherwise, be lent, resold, hired out or otherwise cir-
culated without the publisher's prior consent in any form of binding
or cover than that in which it is published and without a
similar condition including this condition being imposed on the
subsequent purchaser.

For
BERNARD STONE

Contents

9

Introduction

Robert Browning was born in 1812, and died on December 12th, 1889. Long enough ago, one might suppose, for even the most controversial of poets to have found a solid place in the hierarchy. Yet Browning remains an embarrassment to critics. Their pens stumble when they write about him. What are the reasons? Why is his reputation so ambiguous? An introduction to Browning's work must take these questions into account. And it must deal with the unambiguous side of him as well. There is no argument about the extent of Browning's influence. I find, looking through the work of my contemporaries, that borrowings from Browning crop up in the most unexpected places. Here, for example, are the opening lines of a poem by Donald Davie:

> The world of God has turned its two stone faces
> One my way, one yours. Yet we change places
> A little, slowly. After we had halved
> The work between us, those grotesques I carved
> There in the first bays clockwise from the door,
> That was such work as I got credit for
> At York and Beverley: thorn-leaves twined and bent
> To frame some small and human incident
> Domestic or of venery.

> (*To a Brother in the Mystery*)

And here are some from a poem by George MacBeth:

> Was it alive? I often asked myself
> And avoided the answer. I called it something cooking,
> Curled up and rising, soft shapeless matter
> Stuck to my greased sides waiting to be born.

> (*A Confession*)

The debt to Browning is, I think, quite plain in each case. And there are many other poets and poems where it is possible to trace

Browning's influence at work in a more general sense. Indeed, I cannot think of any other nineteenth-century poet whose work is still so much alive in the mid-twentieth. Browning moves within contemporary English and American poetry like yeast in dough. Compared to him, Hopkins and Whitman have played only superficial roles.

It is always tempting, in literary criticism as elsewhere, to move from the known towards the unknown. In Browning's case, the succession is comparatively easy to discuss — it is the work itself which presents difficulties. The inheritance which Browning left to the poets of our own day is something I mean to try and deal with in this essay, but it would be a little perverse to begin the discussion there.

Perhaps, first of all, I should attempt to give some picture of what I think the difficulties really are. What are the things in Browning which fend off modern readers, and unsettle modern critics? Adrian Stokes, in his recent book *The Invitation in Art*, has this to say about the relationship between the poem and the reader:

'A poem, like a picture, properly appreciated, stands away from us as an object on its own, but the poetry that has gripped, the poetry of which it is composed, when read as an unfolding process, combines with corresponding processes in a reader who lends himself.'

Browning, in some curious way, fails to grip. We consider his poems as separate objects; they do not become part of ourselves.

One explanation of this failure — an explanation which does not convince me — puts the blame on the early disaster which Browning suffered in the reception accorded to his first published work, *Pauline*. Certainly the poem itself came to embarrass him in later life, and he reprinted it only with reluctance. Certainly, too, Browning's major works were thenceforward to be impersonations, rather than confessions. Yet how revealing these impersonations are! The germ of a given poem can so often be traced directly to the circumstances of Browning's own life. *Mr. Sludge, 'The Medium'*, for example, and the later and less successful *Prince Hohenstein-Schwangau* are poems which reflect two of the very few points of difference which arose between Browning and his wife — her interest in spiritualism, and particularly in the famous American medium, Daniel Home; and her admiration for Napoleon III. But yet, again, there is Browning's comment to Elizabeth Barrett on the subject of his poetry and hers: 'You speak out, *you*, — I only make men and women speak — give you truth broken into prismatic hues, and fear the pure white light, even if it is in me. . . .' Poets seldom bear witness so candidly against themselves.

Why, then, am I unwilling to accept the evidence? The truth is, that for all the shiftiness of some of his most famous characters, such as Sludge and Bishop Blougram, Browning is not really an author who hides himself. The nearer he steers to very personal things, the more unified his poetry becomes.

He is never more straightforward than in writing of his love for his wife, and his gratitude to her:

> Oh I must feel your brain prompt mine,
>   Your heart anticipate my heart,
> You must be just before, in fine,
>   See and make me see, for your part,
> New depths of the divine!

> But who could have expected this
>   When we two drew together first
> Just for the obvious human bliss,
>   To satisfy life's daily thirst
> With a thing men seldom miss?

> *(By the Fireside)*

In the personal poems, as opposed to the monologues, the famous contortedness of style disappears. Browning's oblique syntax is chiefly a means of creating character. If there is a case to be made against Browning, the charges must not be those of moral cowardice. Those who bring charges of this kind are wilfully blind to what the poet is trying to do, and are unable to accept the technical variousness which allows him to write, now in one style, now in another.

The fact remains that many people dislike Browning's verse. Indifference, in his case, easily becomes hostility. In *The Common Asphodel*, for instance, Robert Graves has this to say:

'Browning exemplifies the poet who appreciated and indulged the popular weakness for profundity, appearing to be profound without really being so, keeping the required illusion by means of various technical devices such as unnecessarily protracted sentences and an over-clipped grammar.'

Mr. Graves is a harsh — some might say a jealous — judge of other poets, but he is not without support in his condemnation. The only thing is that those who are hostile to Browning's work vary somewhat among themselves. Santayana, for example, thought Browning: 'a barbaric genius, a truncated imagination, in thought and art inchoate and ill-digested.' Wilde took a slightly different line. In *Intentions* he delivers himself of a well-known and typically Wildean epigram: 'Meredith is a prose Browning, and so is Browning.' Yet these adverse judgements, though differently phrased, and carrying in each case a slightly different emphasis, do not altogether contradict one another.

The accusation of false profundity is perhaps the most damaging. And here, perhaps, we may ask if Browning intended to be 'profound' in exactly the sense that Graves implies. A great deal of the literature devoted to Browning might lead us to think so. Browning's reputation among his contemporaries was very much of the kind which is accorded to a teacher or sage, and many words have been devoted to discussing the poet's 'message'. This tendency was particularly marked at the period when Browning reached a wide public. Here, for example, is a list of some of the books published in the dozen or so years which lead to the Browning Centenary in 1912: *Robert Browning as a Religious Teacher*, by A. C. Pigou (1901); *The Bible in Browning*, by Minnie G. Machen (1903); *Guidance from Robert Browning in Matters of Faith*, by J. A. Holton (1903); *Browning and Tennyson as Teachers*, by J. M. Robertson (1903); *The Bible in Browning*, by Helene Mayer-Franck (1912); *The Message of Robert Browning*, by A. A. Foster (1912); *Browning's Teachings on Faith, Life and Love*, by W. A. Hind (1912). Some of these books may be less dreadful than the titles suggest — after all, fashions in titles change as much as fashions in everything else — but my list does show the kind of atmosphere which Browning studies used to move in. Nor is this atmosphere entirely dissipated. A recent critic, for instance, asks himself whether *A Toccata of Galuppi's* is 'a damaging attack on the mind'. Topics such as Browning's optimism, or his anti-intellectualism, are still confidently bandied back and forth. But surely all this is beside the point? Browning is not likely to survive because of any message he has to bring us — but then, no poet is. We put up with a far tawdrier intellectual content in the poetry of Yeats, without protesting too much. Leslie Stephen was surely right when he remarked that '[Browning's] sympathy is with the vivid spontaneous intuitions, which disperse the sophistries, and can on occasion override the commonplace rules of conventional morality'.

Or, rather, let me put it another way . . . Browning is not a profound thinker; indeed, he's often rather a muddled one. But there is every reason to believe that he would have agreed with Bergson, who said that 'our thought, in its purely logical form, is incapable of presenting the true nature of life'. Browning's poetry is valuable, not so much for its analysable content, but because it explores the frontier between the rational and the emotional. In Browning's most memorable creations, we see how the logical structure of argument is distorted by the pressure of emotional need. Browning's characters attempt to justify themselves, and at the same moment are laid bare; in a single breath they conceal and yet reveal. It is this will to explore a hitherto uncharted territory which makes Browning something more than the 'infinitely respectable rebel' which Aldous Huxley once called him.

In order to understand where his originality lies, we have to look fairly closely at Browning's most characteristic form, the dramatic monologue. These monologues have been the subject of much misunderstanding. In one way, this is a compliment to the poet. As I hope to show later on, Browning's monologues have become so much part of the heritage of modern verse, that we tend to try to read them precisely as we would read Pound, or Eliot, or even Robert Lowell. And this is not possible. Browning is a nineteenth-century writer, and, in particular, he is a pre-Freudian one. We have to read him with the historical perspective in mind, if we are to get the most out of him. For example, we do not always find that subtlety in the use of symbols which we may feel entitled to expect, and Browning's view of his characters clearly belongs to a slightly different way of thinking about human nature — a difference we accept quite happily when we read Dickens or

Thackeray, but which we find it harder to adjust ourselves to in a poet. But Browning does have one characteristic which links him very closely to the literature of the twentieth century. His interest in the ambiguous, which I've already mentioned, extends to what is *morally* ambiguous, as well as to what is intellectually so. In his excellent study of the dramatic monologue, *The Poetry of Experience*, Robert Langbaum remarks on Browning's use of 'the extraordinary moral position', and the tension between sympathy and judgement which this creates in the reader. Langbaum adds three other observations which seem to me particularly important. First of all, he points out that the speakers in dramatic monologues never change their minds — a point which is easily confirmed by a glance at some of the more famous of Browning's. Secondly, he notes that there is something gratuitous about these monologues — the speakers do not accomplish anything by this flow of utterance; and do not, apparently, hope to do so. Finally, he remarks that the speaker in a dramatic monologue seems to talk 'in order to learn something about himself as a way of learning something about reality. . . . The speaker does not use his utterance to expound a meaning but to pursue one, a meaning which comes to him with the shock of revelation . . . the utterance is in its ultimate effect a private dialogue of the speaker with himself, leading to a private illumination.'

If we accept Langbaum's thesis (and I myself find it convincing) then certain conclusions can be drawn. One is that the imaginary interlocutor, whom Browning has been so much praised for his skill in creating, is really an irrelevance; and where the interlocutor appears, he is to be regarded chiefly as a concession to the Victorian taste for naturalism. I say 'where he appears', because in several of the most famous of Browning's monologues, the interlocutor is not present at all, or is present in such a shadowy way that we scarcely notice him. The speaker in *Abt Vogler*, for example, is talking to himself. So is the discontented 'Italian Person of Quality' in *Up at a Villa — Down in the City*. Caliban, in *Caliban upon Setebos*, is talking to he knows not whom or what.

The idea of the soliloquy as a kind of prison is something which has had a marked effect on modern dramatists. John Osborne's *Inadmissible Evidence* is an inordinately long dramatic monologue which the subsidiary characters try in vain to interrupt. A still closer parallel is provided by some of Beckett's plays. Winnie, in *Happy Days*, is in a situation which in some ways resembles Caliban's. Her strictly limited universe — she is buried in a mound of earth, first up to her waist, then up to her chin — is not really so very much more restricted than Caliban's, who:

> Will sprawl, now that the heat of day is best,
> Flat on his belly in the pit's much mire,
> With elbows wide, fist clenched to prop his chin.

Browning subtitles his poem 'Natural Theology in the Island'; Beckett, I think, might well have called his play 'Natural Theology in the Desert' — the stage directions read: 'Very pompier trompe l'oeil backcloth to represent unbroken plain and sky receding to meet in the far distance.' There are, of course, vast differences. Caliban is a Manichee, who hopes that an evil God can be replaced by some better power. The death of God would be a release. Winnie, like Caliban, is conscious of being watched, but her hopes are pitched less high. She wants the divine attention to remain fixed upon her, as the condition of her own existence:

'Strange feeling that someone is looking at me. I am clear, then dim, then gone, then dim again, then clear again, and so on, back and forth, in and out of some-one's eye.'

Winnie's is a greyer world than Caliban's, and she herself is closer to annihilation and to final nothingness. But some of the resemblances are as striking as the differences. Beckett, the nihilist, is one of the heirs of Browning, the optimist. The incurably 'optimistic' Winnie can almost be regarded as the payment of a debt.

For the moment, however, let us move from this comparison between *Caliban* and *Happy Days* to a consideration of the way in which Browning actually writes. His style is, in some ways, much less advanced than the ideas which his poems embody. Even in *Caliban* the subtlety of the thought is sometimes in conflict with a rather old-fashioned rhetoric. And, in general, the detail of Browning's writing is one of the things which is most apt to repel contemporary readers. Though he can write with immense precision, we too often find, even in his best poems, passages where the writing seems flaccid, unfocused, abstract in the wrong way.

Childe Roland, on the whole one of the most impressive of all Browning's poems, can still dwindle to writing like this:

> For, what with my whole world-wide wandering,
>> What with my search drawn out thro' years, my hope
>> Dwindled into a ghost not fit to cope
> With that obstreperous joy success would bring,
> I hardly tried now to rebuke the spring
>> My heart made, finding failure in its scope.

Browning here is using an inherited diction — inherited, as we know (and can see plainly from *Pauline*) from the work of Shelley. In addition, there is something in Browning's method of writing which prevents him from being always memorable. Browning seems to have written fluently, and to have disliked the labour of revising. He had a technical facility of a special kind. Once he found a 'tune' for a poem, he was apt to stick to it, however forced both diction and rhyming became. Sometimes the results of this effort are strangely apt, as in the often quoted conclusion to *Popularity*:

> Hobbs hints blue, — straight he turtle eats:
>> Nobbs prints blue, — claret crowns his cup:
> Nokes outdares Stokes in azure feats, —
>> Both gorge. Who fished the murex up?
> What porridge had John Keats?

This verse is the end-product of a metaphor which has begun to get out of hand several stanzas earlier. A poet who was a more conscious craftsman would never have teased out the implications at such length.

And yet, I do not mean to imply that Browning was naïve. I think he was very far from that, and some of his technical procedures are among the most interesting things about him. To take the issue of garrulousness first. We have to remember the use to which he puts this flood of words in his monologues — Langbaum has a good phrase for it — the 'superabundance which constitutes the speaker's song'. In many respects, what we find in Browning is a clumsy yet powerful attempt to solve problems which later poets would also have to tackle. Browning, for example, is virtually the first to give serious consideration to the idea that the blank verse medium was exhausted. He has the first glimmerings of a notion that this form, invented as the counterpart to Elizabethan speech patterns, would no longer serve its purpose. His solutions are not radical. They consist, rather, in an attempt to put matters right by legerdemain. In *Mr. Sludge*, for example, there's an insistent 'naturalness' which really isn't natural at all, because it cuts right across the grain of the medium the poet is using:

> But, for God?
> Ay, that's a question! Well sir, since you press —
> (How you do tease the whole thing out of me!
> I don't mean you, you know, when I say 'them':
> Hate you, indeed! But that Miss Stokes, that Judge!
> Enough, enough — with sugar: thank you, sir!)
> Now for it, then! Will you believe me, though!

This I find fascinating, but extremely artificial. Yet it can't be denied that, in tackling the problem so resolutely, Browning invented not a technique, but a 'tone' — a tone which was to be of the utmost service to later writers.

Let us consider for a moment the whole question of the relationship between Browning's fictions, and the things which contemporary poets serve up to us as fact. But perhaps, before I begin this consideration, I may allow myself an aside — to the effect that one of the most striking differences between the great writers of the nineteenth century and ourselves is the decline in the power to make the fictional convincing. To choose a topical example — several critics have recently drawn attention to this failure in the work of Norman Mailer. When Mailer writes reportage, he is convincing — it is all solidly imagined, as well as being brilliantly observed. This is far from being the case with the novels which have followed *The Naked and the Dead*.

The comparison I want to make is between Browning's dramatic monologues, and the 'confessional' poetry of a man like Robert Lowell. Here are a few lines from Browning:

> You, Gigadibs, who, thirty years of age,
> Write stately for Blackwood's Magazine

Believe you see two points in Hamlet's soul
Unseized by the Germans yet — which view you'll print —
Meantime the best you have to show being still
That lively lightsome article we took
Almost for the true Dickens, — what's its name?
'The Slum and Cellar, or Whitechapel life
Limned after dark !' it made me laugh, I know,
And pleased a month, and brought you in ten pounds.

(Bishop Blougram's Apology)

And here is something from Lowell's *Life Studies*:

When I embarked from Italy with my Mother's body,
the whole shoreline of the *Golfo di Genova*
was breaking into fiery flower.
The crazy yellow and azure sea-sleds
blasting like jack-hammers across
the *spumante*-bubbling wake of our liner,
recalled the clashing colours of my Ford.
Mother travelled first-class in the hold,
her *Risorgimento* black and gold casket
was like Napoleon's at the *Invalides* . . .

(Sailing Home from Rapallo)

I can't help noticing what seem to me to be certain similarities of method here: for instance, the thronging 'brand-names'. And the resemblance goes deeper than this. When we look at the two passages side by side, we suddenly realise that Lowell is treating himself as a *persona*, that there is a 'Lowell' who speaks his monologue much as Bishop Blougram does. The method of projection which Browning used for fictional characters, poets now employ to project themselves. The 'confessional' poet, like the heroes of Browning's monologues, talks 'in order to learn something about himself as a way of learning about reality'. The comparison is hammered home in Lowell's case, by the fact that he has also written fictional dramatic monologues, such as the well-known *Falling Asleep Over The Aeneid*.

Besides his development of verse technique to match the monologue-form, there are other things about Browning's writing which are not only deeply characteristic of the poet, but have a relevance to what is happening in poetry to-day. Browning's feeling for the grotesque is one of them; his use of esoteric learning is another. As I hope to show, these two things are linked. But let me begin by noticing, first of all, the fact that Browning's diction (not always perfect) improves enormously in just those parts of his work where the grotesquerie is most apparent:

> How did he like it when the live creatures
>> Tickled and toused and browsed him all over,
> And worm, slug, eft, with serious features,
>> Came in, each one, for his right of trover?
> — When the water-beetle with great blind deaf face
>> Made of her eggs the stately deposit,
> And the newt borrowed just so much of the preface
>> As tiled the top of his black wife's closet?
>
> (Sibrandus Schafnaburgensis)

These lines describe what happens to a book which has been dropped into the damp heart of a hollow plum-tree, and admirably direct and vigorous they are. The description of the water-beetle 'with great blind deaf face' is wonderfully exact. I have always particularly admired the choice of the epithet 'stately' to describe the beetle's method of laying her eggs.

The precision of observation is joined to a precision of scholarship — the rare event is always welcome whether experienced or read about. Browning's delight in the water-beetle's doings is, I think, of very much the same quality as his delight in the musty old account of a Roman murder-trial which provided him with the source for *The Ring and the Book*. Occasionally this use of scholarly detail begins to remind us of Pound. In the late volume, *Parleyings with Certain People of Importance in their Day*, Browning is on the way to creating a private universe of scholarship, very much as Pound does in *The Cantos*.

It is, of course, striking that Browning often finds difficulty in bringing the gleanings of scholarship and the fruits of his own direct observation into a real relationship with one another. The famous series of monologues devoted to painters — *Andrea del*

Sarto, Fra Lippo Lippi, and the rest — have always seemed to me strangely deficient in evidence that Browning had really looked at the work of these artists. There is, instead, plenty of evidence to show that he had given devoted attention to Vasari's *Lives,* and to Baldinucci. Even allowing for the fact that people looked at paintings in quite a different way in the mid-nineteenth century (they preferred subject-matter to 'plastic values') Browning is strangely slow to tell us what the work really looked like. Ruskin's descriptions are more vivid. One of the rare poems that does not bear out this complaint is *The Guardian-Angel,* which is about a picture by Guercino which Browning saw at Fano. This poem has found great favour with many of Browning's commentators, and has fine lines in it, but it is, in general, rather too sentimental for my taste.

Yet despite this defect, I do find that the scholarly side of Browning, and the minutely observant one, can be brought together in a most fascinating way. The thing that links them is Browning's extremism. He pushes both scholarship and observation to their furthest limits, just as he sometimes pushes his plots ('extreme' plots can be found, for example, in *Porphyria's Lover* and in the later and much finer poem, *A Forgiveness,* which was one of Browning's own favourites among his works).

And, in talking of extremism, we have arrived at a most important question, which is to decide what kind of artist Browning really is. In fact, he seems to me to stand at one of the turning points in the history of the arts, and to be an immensely important forerunner of many of the developments which we now see happening around us. Let me give a few examples.

I want to begin by looking at an area of Browning's activity which may seem comparatively marginal. His translations, and especially his translation of the *Agamemnon* of Aeschylus, have not attracted a great deal of attention. Yet I find the language in the *Agamemnon* immensely interesting. Here is a part of a speech by the Herald:

> It suits not to defile a day auspicious
> With ill-announcing speech: distinct each god's due:
> And when a messenger with gloomy visage

22

To a city bear fall'n host's woes — God ward off! —
One popular wound that happens to the city,
And many sacrificed from many households —
Men, scourged by that two-thonged whip Ares loves so,
Double spear-headed curse, bloody yoke-couple —
Of woes like these, doubtless, whoe'er comes weighted,
Him does it suit to sing the Erinues' paian.

Language is being distorted in this, but not gratuitously. Trans-
lations, it seems to me, are usually compromises. The translator
considers his original from several different points of view — literal
meaning, sound-patterns, and the overall design (which is some-
thing different from the literal meaning). He knows he cannot bring
all of these intact into his translation, especially if he is translating
poetry. So he tries to find an acceptable middle way. It is just this
method of translation which Browning rejects in his version of
the *Agamemnon*. English is laid on the altar of Greek, and the
distortion we notice is really the 'Greekness' of imagery and word-
order which Browning has been at such pains to preserve. Now
this is a peculiarly 'modern' thing to do, an 'extremist' thing to do.
It involves a kind of hypertrophy. The artist exaggerates what
interests him, explores it in depth, examines it minutely. One
aspect is fully covered, all the others are ignored.

To illustrate more fully what I mean, here are some lines from a
recent translation of Catullus by Celia and Louis Zukofsky:

Here's to you — hard put to it confecting harmonious lines —
    promises, Alli, ready turns of your offices,
never strummed scabrous tang that rubbing into your name
    hide a quelling of days hiding a life hiding a life.
Who can then, deal you calm plenitude, high Themis, old hymn
    and antique solace, the moon her ray for her pious:
see this felicity, you two, smiling at you with all
    at home whose love in collusion must set all homing . . .

Here language is wrenched (and renewed) by a kind of literalness
which is somewhat different from Browning's — the overriding
desire is to imitate the *sound* of the original as exactly as possible.
But I do find a resemblance. In each, there is an imbalance which

23

is dynamic, but also a feeling of fragmentation, of some wholeness being destroyed.*

I believe that this comparison has a very real relevance to Browning's methods in general. If the *Agamemnon* is seldom discussed by Browning's critics, the same cannot be said for *The Ring and the Book*. One of the things about the poem which has excited the most comment is the disproportion between the basic material — a sordid murder story — and what Browning made of it. Arthur Symons remarks of Browning that 'as a thinker he conceives of humanity not as an aggregate, but as a collection of units'. This remark seems to take on a colouring of irony if we apply it to *The Ring and the Book*. The focus of the epic is suddenly narrowed to compass the actions and the psychology of a small collection of individuals, some of whom, like Pompilia, we may find touching and admirable, but none of whom, not even the Pope, bestrides the world which he or she inhabits. But the thing which, in the end, makes *The Ring and the Book* so impressive as a work of art is just this relentless study of one small thing, one incident. This intensive mining reveals to us the complexity of life. But it also reveals something else. Here, too, we are conscious that a certain precious unity has been shattered. The writer can no longer deal with reality as though it were one seamless web — or, rather, he can only keep the web intact by narrowing reality, making it something smaller if more intense than previous writers had done. The next stage forward from *The Ring and the Book* is Joyce's *Ulysses*. Here, too, we find the epic at grips with the trivial, and Bloom and Molly seem to me the literary offspring of Guido and Pompilia.

Since this is an important point, and perhaps a difficult one, I think I may be forgiven for approaching it again from a slightly

* After writing these words, I consulted Mr. Zukofsky on the point. He has been kind enough to allow me to quote from his reply: 'I don't remember whether in his preface to the Aeschylus or elsewhere (Browning), tells the reader that he means to transliterate in translating, but I've the feeling he said so. This *sense* of it, or rather of Browning's method was not on my mind when I started the Catullus, but of course one always discovers that some wonderful "lunatic" has always arrived "there" before him — Catullus himself, maybe, after Callimachus, and even further back.'

different angle. *The Ring and the Book* is, I think, representative of a tendency to be seen in all the arts in the second half of the nineteenth century and at the beginning of this one. It shows itself especially clearly in music, and has been ably analysed by several critics. They point out, for example, in the work of Richard Strauss, a strange disproportion of means to ends. In the *Sinfonia Domestica*, Strauss brings the panoply of the late-romantic symphony to subject-matter which stands at the farthest extreme from the kind of grandeur inherent in the form. Something similar is at work in the operas of Puccini. The heroic apparatus used by Verdi is adapted to contain and support the fragile sorrows of *Mimi* and of *Madam Butterfly*. The music of this period has a particular liking for the sensational — think of Strauss's *Electra* and of his *Salome*. And we can find a similar quality in Browning. G. K. Chesterton calls *Fears and Scruples* — 'the masterpiece of that excellent but much abused literary quality, Sensationalism' — and is, I think, quite right.

Like the late romantic composers, Browning predicts the developments which are to follow. This can be clearly demonstrated by looking at the way in which he influenced other writers.

Browning's influence is extraordinarily widespread, and is to be found in conservatives and modernists alike. He is as important to Kipling, Masefield, Frost and Hardy as he is to Pound and Eliot. It is interesting to see what each of these very different writers chose to take (or was able to take) from Browning's work. To turn to Kipling first — we are told of the impact which Browning had on the young Kipling (or Beetle) in a well-known passage in *Stalky & Co*. Beetle discovers Browning through having a volume of the poems thrown at his head:

'The quarter-comprehended verses lived and ate with him, as the be-dropped pages shewed. He removed himself from all the world, drifting at large with wondrous Men and Women.'

But when he wanted to repeat the effect, Kipling couldn't resist tidying things up. No one would deny that *The Mary Glocester* is an impressive and moving poem, but it is much more naturalistic than the best of Browning, and we feel the limitations of naturalism in it. The nearest comparison is probably *The Bishop Orders His Tomb at St. Praxed's*, but to understand what it was that Kipling missed in his anxiety to preserve a clear and effective story line, we have to look at something like *Caliban upon Setebos*.

Frost, too, doesn't have quite the courage to take everything that is there to be taken. He, perhaps better than anyone, understood the grotesque side of Browning. There is something of this quality in a poem like *The Witch of Coös*. But here, again, the form is less free than Browning could be. All the same, Frost has qualities which we miss in Browning; a wryness and a subtlety which are usually absent from the older poet.

So far as Hardy is concerned, we find Browning's influence working in yet another way. *The Ring and the Book* undoubtedly made its impress on *The Dynasts*, but Hardy seems to have found the best nourishment for his own poetry in those poems where Browning writes about the love-relationship: in Hardy there are often echoes of things like *Any Wife to Any Husband*.

The most important example of the power of Browning's influence is, however, to be seen in Pound, and it seems to me that a study of Pound's work, and of its relationship to Browning, throws a flood of light on Browning himself, and what he was trying to do. The early Pound imitates Browning's monologues almost slavishly. Here he is at an early stage, in a poem written in 1907. He is still trying to work his way into the form, trying to understand what his model was really up to:

> 'These sell our pictures!!! Oh well,
> They reach me not, touch me some edge or that,
> But reach me not and all my life's become
> One flame that reaches not beyond
> My heart's own hearth,
> Or hides among the ashes there for thee.
> 'Thee'? Oh, 'Thee' is who cometh first
> Out of mine own soul-kin,
> For I am homesick after mine own kind
> And ordinary people touch me not.

> (*In Durance*)

Seven or eight years later, Pound has got the borrowed manner under much tighter control, and has come much closer to Browning in the process:

You'd have men's hearts up from the dust
And tell their secrets, Messire Cino,
Right enough? Then read between the lines of Uc St. Circ,
Solve me the riddle, for you know the tale.

(*Near Perigord*)

When T. S. Eliot remarked, in his introduction to Pound's *Selected Poems* (1935) that '(Pound) is much more modern, in my opinion, when he deals with Italy and Provence, than when he deals with modern life', he was, in an oblique way, paying a compliment to the strength of Browning's genius.

The literary relationship between the two poets is, however, at its most important and interesting at the point when Pound begins to break away:

> Hang it all, Robert Browning,
>   there can be but one 'Sordello'.
> But Sordello, and my Sordello?

(*Canto II*)

It is here, rather than in the imitations, that we see how much Browning had to give. It is not difficult, for instance, to see how much *Mr. Sludge* has contributed to a passage like this, while recognising that the effect is now quite different:

> Sabotage? Yes, he took it up to Manhattan,
> To the big company, and they said: Impossible.
> And he said: I gawt ten thousand dollars tew mak' em,
> And I'm a goin' tew mak' em, and you'll damn well
> *Have* to install'em, awl over the place.

(*Canto XIX*)

But the full fruits of Browning's influence are to be seen in some of the loveliest passages of the whole immense poem:

> Velvet, yellow, unwinged
> clambers, a ball, into its orchis
> and the stair there still broken
> the flat stones of the road, Mt Segur.

27

From Val Cabrere, were two miles of roof to San Bertrand
so that a cat need not set foot in the road
where now is an inn, and bare rafters . . .

(Canto XLVIII)

The first two lines, with their detailed, eccentric observation go
back to the kind of thing I've already examined in a stanza taken
from *Sibrandus Schafnaburgensis*. The oblique syntax, and the homely
image in the penultimate line are also significant.

Pound's colleague and ally, Eliot, also responded to Browning.
Gerontion demonstrates how thoroughly he assimilated the lesson of
the most advanced of the monologues, such as *Caliban* and *Childe
Roland*. Like the protagonists of these two poems, *Gerontion* is a
being suspended, a man outside normal space and time, released to
be himself, and at the same time suffering from the horrors of
disorientation:

> My house is a decayed house,
> And the Jew squats on the windowsill, the owner,
> Spawned in some estaminet of Antwerp,
> Blistered in Brussels, patched and peeled in London.
> The goat coughs at night in the field overhead.
> Rocks, moss, stonecrop, iron, merds.

The last line of this quotation summons up the whole landscape of
Childe Roland:

> As for the grass, it grew as scant as hair
>   In leprosy; thin dry blades pricked the mud
>   Which underneath looked kneaded up with blood.
> One stiff blind horse, his every bone a-stare,
> Stood stupefied, however he came there:
>   Thrust out past service from the devil's stud!

To quote Chesterton once more: '[Childe Roland] is the song of
the beauty of refuse; and Browning was the first to sing it.'

It will be plain, I think, from this series of comparisons, that I
have been trying to use more recent writers as a kind of mirror, in
which Browning's real virtues and importance may be seen
reflected. The difficulties we have with Browning are of a very

special kind. Modern literature has taken too much from him, and has thus drained his work of its original excitement. Much misunderstood in his own time, Browning is now doomed to be misunderstood in ours. From being impenetrable, he has graduated to being obvious. The success of his own experiments has made him seem jejune.

Yet Browning remains a giant. His celebrated optimism, his air (so often reported by biographers) of being well-adjusted to the society in which he found himself — these have tended to obscure the fact that Browning, more than any other Victorian, is responsible for the direction taken by our own literature, and foreshadows many of its characteristics. Browning is a kind of quarry, from which modern poetry continues to be hewn. Like the material which comes out of a quarry, his work may seem to us rough, without form, lack-lustre. It straddles two literary epochs and conforms to the standards of neither. But, for all that, he remains a poet who must be read — one of the very few essential writers of the English nineteenth century. And once we have 'read ourselves in' he is still a poet who is capable of giving great pleasure, who creates a universe for us which we can inhabit and explore.

NOTE ON THE SELECTION

This does not pretend to be a balanced selection from Browning's work. Browning is a writer who needs space for his best effects. I have chosen the poems which interest me most, and which best illustrate my own view of Browning's work and of its significance. Missing 'anthology pieces' are easily available elsewhere.

EDWARD LUCIE-SMITH

SOURCES OF MATTER QUOTED IN THE TEXT

Donald Davie, *To a Brother in the Mystery, New and Selected Poems*, Wesleyan University Press

George MacBeth, 'A Confession', *The Broken Places*, Scorpion Press

Adrian Stokes, *The Invitation in Art*, Tavistock Press

Robert Graves, *The Common Asphodel*, Hamish Hamilton

Robert Langbaum, *The Poetry of Experience*, Chatto and Windus

Samuel Beckett, *Happy Days*, Faber and Faber

Robert Lowell, 'Sailing Home from Rapallo', *Life Studies*, Faber and Faber

Louis and Celia Zukofsky, *Versions of Catullus*, Poetry (Chicago), Volume 105, Number 3, December 1964

Rudyard Kipling, *Stalky & Co.*, Macmillan & Co. Ltd

Ezra Pound, 'In Durance', *Personae*, Faber and Faber

Ezra Pound, 'Near Perigord', *Personae*, Faber and Faber

Ezra Pound, Cantos II, XIX, and XLVIII, *The Cantos of Ezra Pound*, Faber and Faber

T. S. Eliot, 'Gerontion', *Collected Poems*, Faber and Faber

Song

(From *Pippa Passes*)

You'll love me yet!— and I can tarry
  Your love's protracted growing:
June reared that bunch of flowers you carry,
  From seeds of April's sowing.

I plant a heartful now: some seed
  At least is sure to strike,
And yield — what you'll not pluck indeed,
  Not love, but, may be, like.

You'll look at least on love's remains,
  A grave's one violet:
Your look?— that pays a thousand pains.
  What's death? You'll love me yet!

Johannes Agricola in Meditation

There's heaven above, and night by night
  I look right through its gorgeous roof;
No suns and moons though e'er so bright
  Avail to stop me; splendour-proof
  I keep the broods of stars aloof:
For I intend to get to God,
  For 't is to God I speed so fast,
For in God's breast, my own abode,
  Those shoals of dazzling glory, passed,
  I lay my spirit down at last.
I lie where I have always lain,
  God smiles as he has always smiled;

31

Ere suns and moons could wax and wane,
　　Ere stars were thundergirt, or piled
　　The heavens, God thought on me his child;
Ordained a life for me, arrayed
　　Its circumstances every one
To the minutest; ay, God said
　　This head this hand should rest upon
　　Thus, ere he fashioned star or sun.
And having thus created me,
　　Thus rooted me, he bade me grow,
Guiltless for ever, like a tree
　　That buds and blooms, nor seeks to know
　　The law by which it prospers so:
But sure that thought and word and deed
　　All go to swell his love for me,
Me, made because that love had need
　　Of something irreversibly
　　Pledged solely its content to be.
Yes, yes, a tree which must ascend,
　　No poison-gourd foredoomed to stoop.
I have God's warrant, could I blend
　　All hideous sins, as in a cup,
　　To drink the mingled venoms up;
Secure my nature will convert
　　The draught to blossoming gladness fast:
While sweet dews turn to the gourd's hurt,
　　And bloat, and while they bloat it, blast,
　　As from the first its lot was cast.
For as I lie, smiled on, full-fed
　　By unexhausted power to bless,
I gaze below on hell's fierce bed,
　　And those its waves of flame oppress,
　　Swarming in ghastly wretchedness;
Whose life on earth aspired to be
　　One altar-smoke, so pure! — to win
If not love like God's love for me,
　　At least to keep his anger in;
　　And all their striving turned to sin.

Priest, doctor, hermit, monk grown white
    With prayer, the broken-hearted nun,
The martyr, the wan acolyte,
    The incense-swinging child, — undone
    Before God fashioned star or sun !
God, whom I praise ; how could I praise,
    If such as I might understand,
Make out and reckon on his ways,
    And bargain for his love, and stand,
    Paying a price, at his right hand?

Pictor Ignotus

FLORENCE, 15 —

I could have painted pictures like that youth's
    Ye praise so. How my soul springs up ! No bar
Stayed me — ah, thought which saddens while it soothes !
    — Never did fate forbid me, star by star,
To outburst on your night with all my gift
    Of fires from God : nor would my flesh have shrunk
From seconding my soul, with eyes uplift
    And wide to heaven, or, straight like thunder, sunk
To the centre, of an instant ; or around
    Turned calmly and inquisitive, to scan
The licence and the limit, space and bound,
    Allowed to truth made visible in man.
And, like that youth ye praise so, all I saw,
    Over the canvas could my hand have flung,
Each face obedient to its passion's law,
    Each passion clear proclaimed without a tongue ;
Whether Hope rose at once in all the blood,
    A-tiptoe for the blessing of embrace,
Or Rapture drooped the eyes, as when her brood
    Pull down the nesting dove's heart to its place ;
Or Confidence lit swift the forehead up,
    And locked the mouth fast, like a castle braved, —

O human faces, hath it spilt, my cup?
    What did ye give me that I have not saved?
Nor will I say I have not dreamed (how well!)
    Of going — I, in each new picture, — forth,
As, making new hearts beat and bosoms swell,
    To Pope or Kaiser, East, West, South, or North,
Bound for the calmly-satisfied great State,
    Or glad aspiring little burgh, it went,
Flowers cast upon the car which bore the freight,
    Through old streets named afresh from the event,
Till it reached home, where learned age should greet
    My face, and youth, the star not yet distinct
Above his hair, lie learning at my feet! —
    Oh, thus to live, I and my picture, linked
With love about, and praise, till life should end,
    And then not go to heaven, but linger here,
Here on my earth, earth's every man my friend, —
    The thought grew frightful, 't was so wildly dear!
But a voice changed it. Glimpses of such sights
    Have scared me, like the revels through a door
Of some strange house of idols at its rites!
    This world seemed not the world it was before:
Mixed with my loving trusting ones, there trooped
    ... Who summoned those cold faces that begun
To press on me and judge me? Though I stooped
    Shrinking, as from the soldiery a nun,
They drew me forth, and spite of me ... enough!
    These buy and sell our pictures, take and give,
Count them for garniture and household-stuff,
    And where they live needs must our pictures live
And see their faces, listen to their prate,
    Partakers of their daily pettiness,
Discussed of, — 'This I love, or this I hate,
    This likes me more, and this affects me less!'
Wherefore I chose my portion. If at whiles
    My heart sinks, as monotonous I paint
These endless cloisters and eternal aisles
    With the same series, Virgin, Babe and Saint,

With the same cold calm beautiful regard, —
   At least no merchant traffics in my heart;
The sanctuary's gloom at least shall ward
   Vain tongues from where my pictures stand apart:
Only prayer breaks the silence of the shrine
   While, blackening in the daily candle-smoke,
They moulder on the damp wall's travertine,
   'Mid echoes the light footstep never woke.
So, die my pictures ! surely, gently die !
   O youth, men praise so, — holds their praise its worth?
Blown harshly, keeps the trump its golden cry?
   Tastes sweet the water with such specks of earth?

The Bishop Orders His Tomb at
Saint Praxed's Church

ROME, 15 —

Vanity, saith the preacher, vanity !
Draw round my bed: is Anselm keeping back?
Nephews — sons mine . . . ah God, I know not ! Well —
She, men would have to be your mother once,
Old Gandolf envied me, so fair she was !
What's done is done, and she is dead beside,
Dead long ago, and I am Bishop since,
And as she died so must we die ourselves,
And thence ye may perceive the world's a dream.
Life, how and what is it? As here I lie
In this state-chamber, dying by degrees,
Hours and long hours in the dead night, I ask
'Do I live, am I dead?' Peace, peace seems all.
Saint Praxed's ever was the church for peace;
And so, about this tomb of mine. I fought
With tooth and nail to save my niche, ye know:
— Old Gandolf cozened me, despite my care;

Shrewd was that snatch from out the corner South
He graced his carrion with, God curse the same!
Yet still my niche is not so cramped but thence
One sees the pulpit o' the epistle-side,
And somewhat of the choir, those silent seats,
And up into the aery dome where live
The angels, and a sunbeam's sure to lurk:
And I shall fill my slab of basalt there,
And 'neath my tabernacle take my rest,
With those nine columns round me, two and two,
The odd one at my feet where Anselm stands:
Peach-blossom marble all, the rare, the ripe
As fresh-poured red wine of a mighty pulse.
— Old Gandolf with his paltry onion-stone,
Put me where I may look at him! True peach,
Rosy and flawless: how I earned the prize!
Draw close: that conflagration of my church
— What then? So much was saved if aught were missed!
My sons, ye would not be my death? Go dig
The white-grape vineyard where the oil-press stood,
Drop water gently till the surface sink,
And if ye find . . . Ah God, I know not, I! . . .
Bedded in store of rotten fig-leaves soft,
And corded up in a tight olive-frail,
Some lump, ah God, of *lapis lazuli*,
Big as a Jew's head cut off at the nape,
Blue as a vein o'er the Madonna's breast . . .
Sons, all have I bequeathed you, villas, all,
That brave Frascati villa with its bath,
So, let the blue lump poise between my knees,
Like God the Father's globe on both his hands
Ye worship in the Jesu Church so gay,
For Gandolf shall not choose but see and burst!
Swift as a weaver's shuttle fleet our years:
Man goeth to the grave, and where is he?
Did I say basalt for my slab, sons? Black —
'T was ever antique-black I meant! How else
Shall ye contrast my frieze to come beneath?

The bas-relief in bronze ye promised me,
Those Pans and Nymphs ye wot of, and perchance
Some tripod, thyrsus, with a vase or so,
The Saviour at his sermon on the mount,
Saint Praxed in a glory, and one Pan
Ready to twitch the Nymph's last garment off,
And Moses with the tables ... but I know
Ye mark me not! What do they whisper thee,
Child of my bowels, Anselm? Ah, ye hope
To revel down my villas while I gasp
Bricked o'er with beggar's mouldy travertine
Which Gandolf from his tomb-top chuckles at!
Nay, boys, ye love me — all of jasper, then!
'T is jasper ye stand pledged to, lest I grieve
My bath must needs be left behind, alas!
One block, pure green as a pistachio-nut,
There's plenty jasper somewhere in the world —
And have I not Saint Praxed's ear to pray
Horses for ye, and brown Greek manuscripts,
And mistresses with great smooth marbly limbs?
— That's if ye carve my epitaph aright,
Choice Latin, picked phrase, Tully's every word,
No gaudy ware like Gandolf's second line —
Tully, my masters? Ulpian serves his need!
And then how I shall lie through centuries,
And hear the blessed mutter of the mass,
And see God made and eaten all day long,
And feel the steady candle-flame, and taste
Good strong thick stupefying incense-smoke!
For as I lie here, hours of the dead night,
Dying in state and by such slow degrees,
I fold my arms as if they clasped a crook,
And stretch my feet forth straight as stone can point,
And let the bedclothes, for a mortcloth, drop
Into great laps and folds of sculptor's-work:
And as yon tapers dwindle, and strange thoughts
Grow, with a certain humming in my ears,
About the life before I lived this life,

And this life too, popes, cardinals and priests,
Saint Praxed at his sermon on the mount,
Your tall pale mother with her talking eyes,
And new-found agate urns as fresh as day,
And marble's language, Latin pure, discreet,
— Aha, ELUCESCEBAT quoth our friend?
No Tully, said I, Ulpian at the best!
Evil and brief hath been my pilgrimage.
All *lapis*, all, sons! Else I give the Pope
My villas! Will ye ever eat my heart?
Ever your eyes were as a lizard's quick,
They glitter like your mother's for my soul,
Or ye would heighten my impoverished frieze,
Piece out its starved design, and fill my vase
With grapes, and add a vizor and a Term,
And to the tripod ye would tie a lynx
That in his struggle throws the thyrsus down,
To comfort me on my entablature
Whereon I am to lie till I must ask
'Do I live, am I dead?' There, leave me, there!
For ye have stabbed me with ingratitude
To death — ye wish it — God, ye wish it! Stone —
Gritstone, a-crumble! Clammy squares which sweat
As if the corpse they keep were oozing through —
And no more *lapis* to delight the world!
Well go! I bless ye. Fewer tapers there,
But in a row: and, going, turn your backs
— Ay, like departing altar-ministrants,
And leave me in my church, the church for peace,
That I may watch at leisure if he leers —
Old Gandolf, at me, from his onion-stone,
As still he envied me, so fair she was!

Bishop Blougram's Apology

No more wine? then we'll push back chairs and talk.
A final glass for me, though: cool, i' faith!
We ought to have our Abbey back, you see.
It's different, preaching in basilicas,
And doing duty in some masterpiece
Like this of brother Pugin's, bless his heart!
I doubt if they're half baked, those chalk rosettes,
Ciphers and stucco-twiddlings everywhere;
It's just like breathing in a lime-kiln: eh?
These hot long ceremonies of our church
Cost us a little — oh, they pay the price,
You take me — amply pay it! Now, we'll talk.

So, you despise me, Mr. Gigadibs.
No deprecation, — nay, I beg you, sir!
Beside 't is our engagement: don't you know,
I promised, if you'd watch a dinner out,
We'd see truth dawn together? — truth that peeps
Over the glasses' edge when dinner's done,
And body gets its sop and holds its noise
And leaves soul free a little. Now's the time:
Truth's break of day! You do despise me then.
And if I say, 'despise me,' — never fear!
I know you do not in a certain sense —
Not in my arm-chair, for example: here,
I well imagine you respect my place
(*Status, entourage*, worldly circumstance)
Quite to its value — very much indeed:
— Are up to the protesting eyes of you
In pride at being seated here for once —
You'll turn it to such capital account!
When somebody, through years and years to come,
Hints of the bishop, — names me — that's enough:
'Blougram? I knew him' — (into it you slide)
'Dined with him once, a Corpus Christi Day,

All alone, we two; he's a clever man:
And after dinner, — why, the wine you know, —
Oh, there was wine, and good! — what with the wine . . .
'Faith, we began upon all sorts of talk!
He's no bad fellow, Blougram; he had seen
Something of mine he relished, some review:
He's quite above their humbug in his heart,
Half-said as much, indeed — the thing's his trade.
I warrant, Blougram's sceptical at times:
How otherwise? I liked him, I confess!'
Che che, my dear sir, as we say at Rome,
Don't you protest now! It's fair give and take;
You have had your turn and spoken your home-truths:
The hand's mine now, and here you follow suit.

Thus much conceded, still the first fact stays —
You do despise me; your ideal of life
Is not the bishop's: you would not be I.
You would like better to be Goethe, now,
Or Buonaparte, or, bless me, lower still,
Count D'Orsay, — so you did what you preferred,
Spoke as you thought, and, as you cannot help,
Believed or disbelieved, no matter what,
So long as on that point, whate'er it was,
You loosed your mind, were whole and sole yourself.
— That, my ideal never can include,
Upon that element of truth and worth
Never be based! for say they make me Pope —
(They can't — suppose it for our argument!)
Why, there I'm at my tether's end, I've reached
My height, and not a height which pleases you:
An unbelieving Pope won't do, you say.
It's like those eerie stories nurses tell,
Of how some actor on a stage played Death,
With pasteboard crown, sham orb and tinselled dart,
And called himself the monarch of the world;
Then, going in the tire-room afterward,
Because the play was done, to shift himself,

Got touched upon the sleeve familiarly,
The moment he had shut the closet door,
By Death himself. Thus God might touch a Pope
At unawares, ask what his baubles mean,
And whose part he presumed to play just now.
Best be yourself, imperial, plain and true!

So, drawing comfortable breath again,
You weigh and find, whatever more or less
I boast of my ideal realized
Is nothing in the balance when opposed
To your ideal, your grand simple life,
Of which you will not realize one jot.
I am much, you are nothing; you would be all,
I would be merely much: you beat me there.

No, friend, you do not beat me: hearken why!
The common problem, yours, mine, every one's,
Is — not to fancy what were fair in life
Provided it could be, — but, finding first
What may be, then find how to make it fair
Up to our means: a very different thing!
No abstract intellectual plan of life
Quite irrespective of life's plainest laws,
But one, a man, who is man and nothing more,
May lead within a world which (by your leave)
Is Rome or London, not Fool's-paradise.
Embellish Rome, idealize away,
Make paradise of London if you can,
You're welcome, nay, you're wise.

                                    A simile!
We mortals cross the ocean of this world
Each in his average cabin of a life;
The best's not big, the worst yields elbow-room.
Now for our six months' voyage — how prepare?
You come on shipboard with a landsman's list
Of things he calls convenient: so they are!

An India screen is pretty furniture,
A piano-forte is a fine resource,
All Balzac's novels occupy one shelf,
The new edition fifty volumes long;
And little Greek books, with the funny type
They get up well at Leipsic, fill the next:
Go on! slabbed marble, what a bath it makes!
And Parma's pride, the Jerome, let us add!
'T were pleasant could Correggio's fleeting glow
Hang full in face of one where'er one roams,
Since he more than the others brings with him
Italy's self, — the marvellous Modenese! —
Yet was not on your list before, perhaps.
— Alas, friend, here's the agent . . . is't the name?
The captain, or whoever's master here —
You see him screw his face up; what's his cry
Ere you set foot on shipboard? 'Six feet square!'
If you won't understand what six feet mean,
Compute and purchase stores accordingly —
And if, in pique because he overhauls
Your Jerome, piano, bath, you come on board
Bare — why, you cut a figure at the first
While sympathetic landsmen see you off;
Not afterward, when long ere half seas over,
You peep up from your utterly naked boards
Into some snug and well-appointed berth,
Like mine for instance (try the cooler jug —
Put back the other, but don't jog the ice!)
And mortified you mutter 'Well and good;
He sits enjoying his sea-furniture;
'T is stout and proper, and there's store of it:
Though I've the better notion, all agree,
Of fitting rooms up. Hang the carpenter,
Neat ship-shape fixings and contrivances —
I would have brought my Jerome, frame and all!'
And meantime you bring nothing: never mind —
You've proved your artist-nature: what you don't
You might bring, so despise me, as I say.

Now come, let's backward to the starting place.
See my way: we're two college friends, suppose.
Prepare together for our voyage, then;
Each note and check the other in his work, —
Here's mine, a bishop's outfit; criticize!
What's wrong? why won't you be a bishop too?

Why first, you don't believe, you don't and can't,
(Not stately, that is, and fixedly
And absolutely and exclusively)
In any revelation called divine.
No dogmas nail your faith; and what remains
But say so, like the honest man you are?
First, therefore, overhaul theology!
Nay, I too, not a fool, you please to think,
Must find believing every whit as hard:
And if I do not frankly say as much,
The ugly consequence is clear enough.

Now wait, my friend: well, I do not believe —
If you'll accept no faith that is not fixed,
Absolute and exclusive, as you say.
You're wrong — I mean to prove it in due time.
Meanwhile, I know where difficulties lie
I could not, cannot solve, nor ever shall,
So give up hope accordingly to solve —
(To you, and over the wine). Our dogmas then
With both of us, though in unlike degree,
Missing full credence — overboard with them!
I mean to meet you on your own premise:
Good, there go mine in company with yours!

And now what are we? unbelievers both,
Calm and complete, determinately fixed
To-day, to-morrow and for ever, pray?
You'll guarantee me that? Not so, I think!

In no wise! all we've gained is, that belief,
As unbelief before, shakes us by fits,
Confounds us like its predecessor. Where's
The gain? how can we guard our unbelief,
Make it bear fruit to us? — the problem here.
Just when we are safest, there's a sunset-touch,
A fancy from a flower-bell, some one's death,
A chorus-ending from Euripides, —
And that's enough for fifty hopes and fears
As old and new at once as nature's self,
To rap and knock and enter in our soul,
Take hands and dance there, a fantastic ring,
Round the ancient idol, on his base again, —
The grand Perhaps! We look on helplessly.
There the old misgivings, crooked questions are —
This good God, — what he could do, if he would,
Would, if he could — then must have done long since:
If so, when, where and how? some way must be, —
Once feel about, and soon or late you hit
Some sense, in which it might be, after all.
Why not, 'The Way, the Truth, the Life?'

                                              — That way
Over the mountain, which who stands upon
Is apt to doubt if it be meant for a road;
While, if he views it from the waste itself,
Up goes the line there, plain from base to brow,
Not vague, mistakeable! what's a break or two
Seen from the unbroken desert either side?
And then (to bring in fresh philosophy)
What if the breaks themselves should prove at last
The most consummate of contrivances
To train a man's eye, teach him what is faith?
And so we stumble at truth's very test!
All we have gained then by our unbelief
Is a life of doubt diversified by faith,
For one of faith diversified by doubt:
We called the chess-board white, — we call it black.

44

'Well,' you rejoin, 'the end's no worse, at least;
We've reason for both colours on the board:
Why not confess then, where I drop the faith
And you the doubt, that I'm as right as you?'

Because, friend, in the next place, this being so,
And both things even, — faith and unbelief
Left to a man's choice, — we'll proceed a step,
Returning to our image, which I like.

A man's choice, yes — but a cabin-passenger's —
The man made for the special life o' the world —
Do you forget him? I remember though!
Consult our ship's conditions and you find
One and but one choice suitable to all;
The choice, that you unluckily prefer,
Turning things topsy-turvy — they or it
Going to the ground. Belief or unbelief
Bears upon life, determines its whole course,
Begins at its beginning. See the world
Such as it is, — you made it not, nor I;
I mean to take it as it is, — and you,
Not so you'll take it, — though you get nought else.
I know the special kind of life I like,
What suits the most my idiosyncrasy,
Brings out the best of me and bears me fruit
In power, peace, pleasantness and length of days.
I find that positive belief does this
For me, and unbelief, no whit of this.
— For you, it does, however? — that, we'll try!
'T is clear, I cannot lead my life, at least,
Induce the world to let me peaceably,
Without declaring at the outset, 'Friends,
I absolutely and peremptorily
Believe!' — I say, faith is my waking life:
One sleeps, indeed, and dreams at intervals,
We know, but waking's the main point with us
And my provision's for life's waking part.

Accordingly, I use heart, head and hand
All day, I build, scheme, study, and make friends;
And when night overtakes me, down I lie,
Sleep, dream a little, and get done with it,
The sooner the better, to begin afresh.
What's midnight doubt before the dayspring's faith?
You, the philosopher, that disbelieve,
That recognize the night, give dreams their weight —
To be consistent you should keep your bed,
Abstain from healthy acts that prove you man,
For fear you drowse perhaps at unawares!
And certainly at night you'll sleep and dream,
Live through the day and bustle as you please.
And so you live to sleep as I to wake,
To unbelieve as I to still believe?
Well, and the common sense o' the world calls you
Bed-ridden, — and its good things come to me.
Its estimation, which is half the fight,
That's the first-cabin comfort I secure:
The next . . . but you perceive with half an eye!
Come, come, it's best believing, if we may;
You can't but own that!

                      Next, concede again,
If once we choose belief, on all accounts
We can't be too decisive in our faith,
Conclusive and exclusive in its terms,
To suit the world which gives us the good things.
In every man's career are certain points
Whereon he dares not be indifferent;
The world detects him clearly, if he dare,
As baffled at the game, and losing life.
He may care little or he may care much
For riches, honour, pleasure, work, repose,
Since various theories of life and life's
Success are extant which might easily
Comport with either estimate of these;
And whoso chooses wealth or poverty,

46

Labour or quiet, is not judged a fool
Because his fellow would choose otherwise:
We let him choose upon his own account
So long as he's consistent with his choice.
But certain points, left wholly to himself,
When once a man has arbitrated on,
We say he must succeed there or go hang.
Thus, he should wed the woman he loves most
Or needs most, whatsoe'er the love or need —
For he can't wed twice. Then, he must avouch,
Or follow, at the least, sufficiently,
The form of faith his conscience holds the best,
Whate'er the process of conviction was:
For nothing can compensate his mistake
On such a point, the man himself being judge:
He cannot wed twice, nor twice lose his soul.

Well now, there's one great form of Christian faith
I happened to be born in — which to teach
Was given me as I grew up, on all hands,
As best and readiest means of living by;
The same on examination being proved
The most pronounced moreover, fixed, precise
And absolute form of faith in the whole world —
Accordingly, most potent of all forms
For working on the world. Observe, my friend!
Such as you know me, I am free to say,
In these hard latter days which hamper one,
Myself — by no immoderate exercise
Of intellect and learning, but the tact
To let external forces work for me,
— Bid the street's stones be bread and they are bread;
Bid Peter's creed, or rather, Hildebrand's,
Exalt me o'er my fellows in the world
And make my life an ease and joy and pride;
It does so, — which for me's a great point gained,
Who have a soul and body that exact
A comfortable care in many ways.

There's power in me and will to dominate
Which I must exercise, they hurt me else:
In many ways I need mankind's respect,
Obedience, and the love that's born of fear:
While at the same time, there's a taste I have,
A toy of soul, a titillating thing,
Refuses to digest these dainties crude.
The naked life is gross till clothed upon:
I must take what men offer, with a grace
As though I would not, could I help it, take!
An uniform I wear though over-rich —
Something imposed on me, no choice of mine;
No fancy-dress worn for pure fancy's sake
And despicable therefore! now folk kneel
And kiss my hand — of course the Church's hand.
Thus I am made, thus life is best for me,
And thus that it should be I have procured;
And thus it could not be another way,
I venture to imagine.

                    You'll reply,
So far my choice, no doubt, is a success;
But were I made of better elements,
With nobler instincts, purer tastes, like you,
I hardly would account the thing success
Though it did all for me I say.

                    But, friend,
We speak of what is; not of what might be,
And how't were better if't were otherwise.
I am the man you see here plain enough:
Grant I'm a beast, why, beasts must lead beasts' lives!
Suppose I own at once to tail and claws;
The tailless man exceeds me: but being tailed
I'll lash out lion fashion, and leave apes
To dock their stump and dress their haunches up.
My business is not to remake myself,
But make the absolute best of what God made.

Or — our first simile — though you prove me doomed
To a viler berth still, to the steerage-hole,
The sheep-pen or the pig-stye, I should strive
To make what use of each were possible;
And as this cabin gets upholstery,
That hutch should rustle with sufficient straw.

But, friend, I don't acknowledge quite so fast
I fail of all your manhood's lofty tastes
Enumerated so complacently,
On the mere ground that you forsooth can find
In this particular life I choose to lead
No fit provision for them. Can you not?
Say you, my fault is I address myself
To grosser estimators than should judge?
And that's no way of holding up the soul,
Which, nobler, needs men's praise perhaps, yet knows
One wise man's verdict outweighs all the fools' —
Would like the two, but, forced to choose, takes that.
I pine among my million imbeciles
(You think) aware some dozen men of sense
Eye me and know me, whether I believe
In the last winking Virgin, as I vow,
And am a fool, or disbelieve in her
And am a knave, — approve in neither case,
Withhold their voices though I look their way:
Like Verdi when, at his worst opera's end
(The thing they gave at Florence, — what's its name?)
While the mad houseful's plaudits near out-bang
His orchestra of salt-box, tongs and bones,
He looks through all the roaring and the wreaths
Where sits Rossini patient in his stall.

Nay, friend, I meet you with an answer here —
That even your prime men who appraise their kind
Are men still, catch a wheel within a wheel,
See more in a truth than the truth's simple self,
Confuse themselves. You see lads walk the street

Sixty the minute; what's to note in that?
You see one lad o'erstride a chimney-stack;
Him you must watch — he's sure to fall, yet stands!
Our interest's on the dangerous edge of things.
The honest thief, the tender murderer,
The superstitious atheist, demirep
That loves and saves her soul in new French books —
We watch while these in equilibrium keep
The giddy line midway: one step aside,
They're classed and done with. I, then, keep the line
Before your sages, — just the men to shrink
From the gross weights, coarse scales and labels broad
You offer their refinement. Fool or knave?
Why needs a bishop be a fool or knave
When there's a thousand diamond weights between?
So, I enlist them. Your picked twelve, you'll find,
Profess themselves indignant, scandalized
At thus being held unable to explain
How a superior man who disbelieves
May not believe as well: that's Schelling's way!
It's through my coming in the tail of time,
Nicking the minute with a happy tact.
Had I been born three hundred years ago
They'd say, 'What's strange? Blougram of course believes;'
And, seventy years since, 'disbelieves of course.'
But now, 'He may believe; and yet, and yet
How can he?' All eyes turn with interest.
Whereas, step off the line on either side —
You, for example, clever to a fault,
The rough and ready man who write apace,
Read somewhat seldomer, think perhaps even less —
You disbelieve! Who wonders and who cares?
Lord So-and-so — his coat bedropped with wax,
All Peter's chains about his waist, his back
Brave with the needlework of Noodledom —
Believes! Again, who wonders and who cares?
But I, the man of sense and learning too,
The able to think yet act, the this, the that,

50

I, to believe at this late time of day !
Enough ; you see, I need not fear contempt.

  — Except it's yours ! Admire me as these may,
You don't. But whom at least do you admire?
Present your own perfection, your ideal,
Your pattern man for a minute — oh, make haste,
Is it Napoleon you would have us grow?
Concede the means ; allow his head and hand,
(A large concession, clever as you are)
Good ! In our common primal element
Of unbelief (we can't believe, you know —
We're still at that admission, recollect !)
Where do you find — apart from, towering o'er
The secondary temporary aims
Which satisfy the gross taste you despise —
Where do you find his star? — his crazy trust
God knows through what or in what? it's alive
And shines and leads him, and that's all we want.
Have we aught in our sober night shall point
Such ends as his were, and direct the means
Of working out our purpose straight as his,
Nor bring a moment's trouble on success
With after-care to justify the same?
— Be a Napoleon, and yet disbelieve —
Why, the man's mad, friend, take his light away !
What's the vague good o' the world, for which you dare
With comfort to yourself blow millions up?
We neither of us see it ! we do see
The blown-up millions — spatter of their brains
And writhing of their bowels and so forth
In that bewildering entanglement
Of horrible eventualities
Past calculation to the end of time !
Can I mistake for some clear word of God
(Which were my ample warrant for it all)
His puff of hazy instinct, idle talk,
'The State, that's I,' quack-nonsense about crowns,

And (when one beats the man to his last hold)
A vague idea of setting things to rights,
Policing people efficaciously,
More to their profit, most of all to his own;
The whole to end that dismallest of ends
By an Austrian marriage, cant to us the Church,
And resurrection of the old *régime*?
Would I, who hope to live a dozen years,
Fight Austerlitz for reasons such and such?
No : for, concede me but the merest chance
Doubt may be wrong — there's judgment, life to come!
With just that chance, I dare not. Doubt proves right?
This present life is all? — you offer me
Its dozen noisy years, without a chance
That wedding an archduchess, wearing lace,
And getting called by divers new-coined names,
Will drive off ugly thoughts and let me dine,
Sleep, read and chat in quiet as I like!
Therefore I will not.

                              Take another case;
Fit up the cabin yet another way.
What say you to the poets? shall we write
Hamlet, Othello — make the world our own,
Without a risk to run of either sort?
I can't! — to put the strongest reason first.
'But try,' you urge, 'the trying shall suffice;
The aim, if reached or not, makes great the life:
Try to be Shakespeare, leave the rest to fate!'
Spare my self-knowledge — there's no fooling me!
If I prefer remaining my poor self,
I say so not in self-dispraise but praise.
If I'm a Shakespeare, let the well alone;
Why should I try to be what now I am?
If I'm no Shakespeare, as too probable, —
His power and consciousness and self-delight
And all we want in common, shall I find —
Trying for ever? while on points of taste

Wherewith, to speak it humbly, he and I
Are dowered alike — I'll ask you, I or he,
Which in our two lives realizes most?
Much, he imagined — somewhat, I possess.
He had the imagination; stick to that!
Let him say, 'In the face of my soul's works
Your world is worthless and I touch it not
Lest I should wrong them' — I'll withdraw my plea.
But does he say so? look upon his life!
Himself, who only can, gives judgment there.
He leaves his towers and gorgeous palaces
To build the trimmest house in Stratford town;
Saves money, spends it, owns the worth of things,
Giulio Romano's pictures, Dowland's lute;
Enjoys a show, respects the puppets, too,
And none more, had he seen its entry once,
Than 'Pandulph, of fair Milan cardinal.'
Why then should I who play that personage,
The very Pandulph Shakespeare's fancy made,
Be told that had the poet chanced to start
From where I stand now (some degree like mine
Being just the goal he ran his race to reach)
He would have run the whole race back, forsooth,
And left being Pandulph, to begin write plays?
Ah, the earth's best can be but the earth's best!
Did Shakespeare live, he could but sit at home
And get himself in dreams the Vatican,
Greek busts, Venetian paintings, Roman walls,
And English books, none equal to his own,
Which I read, bound in gold (he never did).
— Terni's fall, Naples' bay and Gothard's top —
Eh, friend? I could not fancy one of these;
But, as I pour this claret, there they are:
I've gained them — crossed St. Gothard last July
With ten mules to the carriage and a bed
Slung inside; is my hap the worse for that?
We want the same things, Shakespeare and myself,
And what I want, I have: he, gifted more,

Could fancy he too had them when he liked,
But not so thoroughly that, if fate allowed,
He would not have them also in my sense.
We play one game; I send the ball aloft
No less adroitly that of fifty strokes
Scarce five go o'er the wall so wide and high
Which sends them back to me: I wish and get.
He struck balls higher and with better skill,
But at a poor fence level with his head,
And hit — his Stratford house, a coat of arms,
Successful dealings in his grain and wool, —
While I receive heaven's incense in my nose
And style myself the cousin of Queen Bess.
Ask him, if this life's all, who wins the game?

Believe — and our whole argument breaks up.
Enthusiasm's the best thing, I repeat;
Only, we can't command it; fire and life
Are all, dead matter's nothing, we agree:
And be it a mad dream or God's very breath,
The fact's the same, — belief's fire, once in us,
Makes of all else mere stuff to show itself:
We penetrate our life with such a glow
As fire lends wood and iron — this turns steel,
That burns to ash — all's one, fire proves its power
For good or ill, since men call flare success.
But paint a fire, it will not therefore burn.
Light one in me, I'll find it food enough!
Why, to be Luther — that's a life to lead,
Incomparably better than my own.
He comes, reclaims God's earth for God, he says,
Sets up God's rule again by simple means,
Re-opens a shut book, and all is done.
He flared out in the flaring of mankind;
Such Luther's luck was: how shall such be mine?
If he succeeded, nothing's left to do:
And if he did not altogether — well,
Strauss is the next advance. All Strauss should be

I might be also. But to what result?
He looks upon no future : Luther did.
What can I gain on the denying side?
Ice makes no conflagration. State the facts,
Read the text right, emancipate the world —
The emancipated world enjoys itself
With scarce a thank-you : Blougram told it first
It could not owe a farthing, — not to him
More than Saint Paul ! 't would press its pay, you think?
Then add there's still that plaguy hundredth chance
Strauss may be wrong. And so a risk is run —
For what gain? not for Luther's, who secured
A real heaven in his heart throughout his life,
Supposing death a little altered things.

   'Ay, but since really you lack faith,' you cry,
'You run the same risk really on all sides,
In cool indifference as bold unbelief.
As well be Strauss as swing 'twixt Paul and him.
It's not worth having, such imperfect faith,
No more available to do faith's work
Than unbelief like mine. Whole faith, or none !'

   Softly, my friend ! I must dispute that point.
Once own the use of faith, I'll find you faith.
We're back on Christian ground. You call for faith :
I show you doubt, to prove that faith exists.
The more of doubt, the stronger faith, I say,
If faith o'ercomes doubt. How I know it does?
By life and man's free will, God gave for that !
To mould life as we choose it, shows our choice :
That's our one act, the previous work's his own.
You criticize the soul? it reared this tree —
This broad life and whatever fruit it bears !
What matter though I doubt at every pore,
Head-doubts, heart-doubts, doubts at my fingers' ends,
Doubts in the trivial work of every day,
Doubts at the very bases of my soul

In the grand moments when she probes herself —
If finally I have a life to show,
The thing I did, brought out in evidence
Against the thing done to me underground
By hell and all its brood, for aught I know?
I say, whence sprang this? shows it faith or doubt?
All's doubt in me; where's break of faith in this?
It is the idea, the feeling and the love,
God means mankind should strive for and show forth
Whatever be the process to that end, —
And not historic knowledge, logic sound,
And metaphysical acumen, sure!
'What think ye of Christ,' friend? when all's done and said,
Like you this Christianity or not?
It may be false, but will you wish it true?
Has it your vote to be so if it can?
Trust you an instinct silenced long ago
That will break silence and enjoin you love
What mortified philosophy is hoarse,
And all in vain, with bidding you despise?
If you desire faith — then you've faith enough:
What else seeks God — nay, what else seek ourselves?
You form a notion of me, we'll suppose,
On hearsay; it's a favourable one:
'But still' (you add), 'there was no such good man,
Because of contradiction in the facts.
One proves, for instance, he was born in Rome,
This Blougram; yet throughout the tales of him
I see he figures as an Englishman.'
Well, the two things are reconcileable.
But would I rather you discovered that,
Subjoining — 'Still, what matter though they be?
Blougram concerns me nought, born here or there.'

Pure faith indeed — you know not what you ask!
Naked belief in God the Omnipotent,
Omniscient, Omnipresent, sears too much
The sense of conscious creatures to be borne.

It were the seeing him, no flesh shall dare.
Some think, Creation's meant to show him forth:
I say it's meant to hide him all it can,
And that's what all the blessed evil's for.
Its use in Time is to environ us,
Our breath, our drop of dew, with shield enough
Against that sight till we can bear its stress.
Under a vertical sun, the exposed brain
And lidless eye and disemprisoned heart
Less certainly would wither up at once
Than mind, confronted with the truth of him.
But time and earth case-harden us to live;
The feeblest sense is trusted most; the child
Feels God a moment, ichors o'er the place,
Plays on and grows to be a man like us.
With me, faith means perpetual unbelief
Kept quiet like the snake 'neath Michael's foot
Who stands calm just because he feels it writhe.
Or, if that's too ambitious, — here's my box —
I need the excitation of a pinch
Threatening the torpor of the inside-nose
Nigh on the imminent sneeze that never comes.
'Leave it in peace' advise the simple folk:
Make it aware of peace by itching-fits,
Say I — let doubt occasion still more faith!

You'll say, once all believed, man, woman, child,
In that dear middle-age these noodles praise.
How you'd exult if I could put you back
Six hundred years, blot out cosmogony,
Geology, ethnology, what not,
(Greek endings, each the little passing-bell
That signifies some faith's about to die),
And set you square with Genesis again, —
When such a traveller told you his last news,
He saw the ark a-top of Ararat
But did not climb there since 't was getting dusk
And robber-bands infest the mountain's foot!

How should you feel, I ask, in such an age,
How act? As other people felt and did;
With soul more blank than this decanter's knob,
Believe — and yet lie, kill, rob, fornicate
Full in belief's face, like the beast you'd be!

No, when the fight begins within himself,
A man's worth something. God stoops o'er his head,
Satan looks up between his feet — both tug —
He's left, himself, i' the middle: the soul wakes
And grows. Prolong that battle through his life!
Never leave growing till the life to come!
Here, we've got callous to the Virgin's winks
That used to puzzle people wholesomely:
Men have outgrown the shame of being fools.
What are the laws of nature, not to bend
If the Church bid them? — brother Newman asks.
Up with the Immaculate Conception, then —
On to the rack with faith! — is my advice.
Will not that hurry us upon our knees,
Knocking our breasts, 'It can't be — yet it shall!
Who am I, the worm, to argue with my Pope?
Low things confound the high things!' and so forth.
That's better than acquitting God with grace
As some folk do. He's tried — no case is proved,
Philosophy is lenient — he may go!

You'll say, the old system's not so obsolete
But men believe still: ay, but who and where?
King Bomba's lazzaroni foster yet
The sacred flame, so Antonelli writes;
But even of these, what ragamuffin saint
Believes God watches him continually,
As he believes in fire that it will burn,
Or rain that it will drench him? Break fire's law,
Sin against rain, although the penalty
Be just a singe or soaking? 'No,' he smiles;
'Those laws are laws that can enforce themselves.'

The sum of all is — yes, my doubt is great,
My faith's still greater, then my faith's enough.
I have read much, thought much, experienced much,
Yet would die rather than avow my fear
The Naples' liquefaction may be false,
When set to happen by the palace-clock
According to the clouds or dinner-time.
I hear you recommend, I might at least
Eliminate, decrassify my faith
Since I adopt it; keeping what I must
And leaving what I can — such points as this.
I won't — that is I can't throw one away.
Supposing there's no truth in what I hold
About the need of trial to man's faith,
Still, when you bid me purify the same,
To such a process I discern no end.
Clearing off one excrescence to see two,
There's ever a next in size, now grown as big,
That meets the knife: I cut and cut again!
First cut the Liquefaction, what comes last
But Fichte's clever cut at God himself?
Experimentalize on sacred things!
I trust nor hand nor eye nor heart nor brain
To stop betimes: they all get drunk alike.
The first step, I am master not to take.

You'd find the cutting-process to your taste
As much as leaving growths of lies unpruned,
Nor see more danger in it, — you retort.
Your taste's worth mine; but my taste proves more wise
When we consider that the steadfast hold
On the extreme end of the chain of faith
Gives all the advantage, makes the difference
With the rough purblind mass we seek to rule:
We are their lords, or they are free of us,
Just as we tighten or relax our hold.
So, other matters equal, we'll revert
To the first problem —which, if solved my way

And thrown into the balance, turns the scale —
How we may lead a comfortable life,
How suit our luggage to the cabin's size.

    Of course you are remarking all this time
How narrowly and grossly I view life,
Respect the creature-comforts, care to rule
The masses, and regard complacently
'The cabin,' in our old phrase. Well, I do.
I act for, talk for, live for this world now,
As this world prizes action, life and talk:
No prejudice to what next world may prove,
Whose new laws and requirements, my best pledge
To observe then, is that I observe these now,
Shall do hereafter what I do meanwhile.
Let us concede (gratuitously though)
Next life relieves the soul of body, yields
Pure spiritual enjoyment: well, my friend,
Why lose this life i' the meantime, since its use
May be to make the next life more intense?

    Do you know, I have often had a dream
(Work it up in your next month's article)
Of man's poor spirit in its progress, still
Losing true life for ever and a day
Through ever trying to be and ever being —
In the evolution of successive spheres —
Before its actual sphere and place of life,
Halfway into the next, which having reached,
It shoots with corresponding foolery
Halfway into the next still, on and off!
As when a traveller, bound from North to South,
Scouts fur in Russia: what's its use in France?
In France spurns flannel: where's its need in Spain:
In Spain drops cloth, too cumbrous for Algiers!
Linen goes next, and last the skin itself,
A superfluity at Timbuctoo.
When, through his journey, was the fool at ease?

I'm at ease now, friend; worldly in this world,
I take and like its way of life; I think
My brothers, who administer the means,
Live better for my comfort — that's good too;
And God, if he pronounce upon such life,
Approves my service, which is better still.
If he keep silence, — why, for you or me
Or that brute beast pulled-up in to-day's 'Times,'
What odds is't, save to ourselves, what life we lead?

You meet me at this issue: you declare, —
All special-pleading done with — truth is truth,
And justifies itself by undreamed ways.
You don't fear but it's better, if we doubt,
To say so, act up to our truth perceived
However feebly. Do then, — act away!
'T is there I'm on the watch for you. How one acts
Is, both of us agree, our chief concern:
And how you'll act is what I fain would see
If, like the candid person you appear,
You dare to make the most of your life's scheme
As I of mine, live up to its full law
Since there's no higher law that counterchecks.
Put natural religion to the test
You've just demolished the revealed with — quick,
Down to the root of all that checks your will,
All prohibition to lie, kill and thieve,
Or even to be an atheistic priest!
Suppose a pricking to incontinence —
Philosophers deduce you chastity
Or shame, from just the fact that at the first
Whoso embraced a woman in the field,
Threw club down and forewent his brains beside,
So, stood a ready victim in the reach
Of any brother savage, club in hand;
Hence saw the use of going out of sight
In wood or cave to prosecute his loves:
I read this in a French book t' other day.

Does law so analysed coerce you much?
Oh, men spin clouds of fuzz where matters end,
But you who reach where the first thread begins,
You'll soon cut that ! — which means you can, but won't,
Through certain instincts, blind, unreasoned-out,
You dare not set aside, you can't tell why,
But there they are, and so you let them rule.
Then, friend, you seem as much a slave as I,
A liar, conscious coward and hypocrite,
Without the good the slave expects to get,
In case he has a master after all !
You own your instincts? why, what else do I,
Who want, am made for, and must have a God
Ere I can be aught, do aught? — no mere name
Want, but the true thing with what proves its truth,
To wit, a relation from that thing to me,
Touching from head to foot — which touch I feel,
And with it take the rest, this life of ours !
I live my life here ; yours you dare not live.

    — Not as I state it, who (you please subjoin)
Disfigure such a life and call it names,
While, to your mind, remains another way
For simple men : knowledge and power have rights,
But ignorance and weakness have rights too.
There needs no crucial effort to find truth
If here or there or anywhere about :
We ought to turn each side, try hard and see,
And if we can't, be glad we've earned at least
The right, by one laborious proof the more,
To graze in peace earth's pleasant pasturage.
Men are not angels, neither are they brutes :
Something we may see, all we cannot see.
What need of lying? I say, I see all,
And swear to each detail the most minute
In what I think a Pan's face — you, mere cloud :
I swear I hear him speak and see him wink,
For fear, if once I drop the emphasis,

Mankind may doubt there's any cloud at all.
You take the simple life — ready to see,
Willing to see (for no cloud's worth a face) —
And leaving quiet what no strength can move,
And which, who bids you move? who has the right?
I bid you; but you are God's sheep, not mine:
'*Pastor est tui Dominus.*' You find
In this the pleasant pasture of our life
Much you may eat without the least offence,
Much you don't eat because your maw objects,
Much you would eat but that your fellow-flock
Open great eyes at you and even butt,
And thereupon you like your mates so well
You cannot please yourself, offending them;
Though when they seem exorbitantly sheep,
You weigh your pleasure with their butts and bleats
And strike the balance. Sometimes certain fears
Restrain you, real checks since you find them so;
Sometimes you please yourself and nothing checks:
And thus you graze through life with not one lie,
And like it best.

              But do you, in truth's name?
If so, you beat — which means you are not I —
Who needs must make earth mine and feed my fill
Not simply unbutted at, unbickered with,
But motioned to the velvet of the sward
By those obsequious wethers' very selves.
Look at me, sir; my age is double yours:
At yours, I knew beforehand, so enjoyed,
What now I should be — as, permit the word,
I pretty well imagine your whole range
And stretch of tether twenty years to come.
We both have minds and bodies much alike:
In truth's name, don't you want my bishopric,
My daily bread, my influence and my state?
You're young. I'm old; you must be old one day;
Will you find then, as I do hour by hour,

Women their lovers kneel to, who cut curls
From your fat lap-dog's ear to grace a brooch —
Dukes, who petition just to kiss your ring —
With much beside you know or may conceive?
Suppose we die to-night : well, here am I,
Such were my gains, life bore this fruit to me,
While writing all the same my articles
On music, poetry, the fictile vase
Found at Albano, chess, Anacreon's Greek.
But you — the highest honour in your life,
The thing you'll crown yourself with, all your days,
Is — dining here and drinking this last glass
I pour you out in sign of amity
Before we part for ever. Of your power
And social influence, worldly worth in short,
Judge what's my estimation by the fact,
I do not condescend to enjoin, beseech,
Hint secrecy on one of all these words !
You're shrewd and know that should you publish one
The world would brand the lie — my enemies first,
Who'd sneer — 'the bishop's an arch-hypocrite
And knave perhaps, but not so frank a fool.'
Whereas I should not dare for both my ears
Breathe one such syllable, smile one such smile,
Before the chaplain who reflects myself —
My shade's so much more potent than your flesh.
What's your reward, self-abnegating friend?
Stood you confessed of those exceptional
And privileged great natures that dwarf mine —
A zealot with a mad ideal in reach,
A poet just about to print his ode,
A statesman with a scheme to stop this war,
An artist whose religion is his art —
I should have nothing to object : such men
Carry the fire, all things grow warm to them,
Their drugget's worth my purple, they beat me.
But you, — you're just as little those as I —
You, Gigadibs, who, thirty years of age,

Write statedly for Blackwood's Magazine,
Believe you see two points in Hamlet's soul
Unseized by the Germans yet — which view you'll print —
Meantime the best you have to show being still
That lively lightsome article we took
Almost for the true Dickens, — what's its name?
'The Slum and Cellar, or Whitechapel life
Limned after dark !' it made me laugh, I know,
And pleased a month, and brought you in ten pounds.
— Success I recognize and compliment,
And therefore give you, if you choose, three words
(The card and pencil-scratch is quite enough)
Which whether here, in Dublin or New York,
Will get you, prompt as at my eyebrow's wink,
Such terms as never you aspired to get
In all our own reviews and some not ours.
Go write your lively sketches ! be the first
'Blougram, or The Eccentric Confidence' —
Or better simply say, 'The Outward-bound.'
Why, men as soon would throw it in my teeth
As copy and quote the infamy chalked broad
About me on the church-door opposite.
You will not wait for that experience though,
I fancy, howsoever you decide,
To discontinue — not detesting, not
Defaming, but at least — despising me !

————————

Over his wine so smiled and talked his hour
Sylvester Blougram, styled *in partibus*
Episcopus, nec non — (the deuce knows what
It's changed to by our novel hierarchy)
With Gigadibs the literary man,
Who played with spoons, explored his plate's design,
And ranged the olive-stones about its edge,
While the great bishop rolled him out a mind
Long crumpled, till creased consciousness lay smooth.

For Blougram, he believed, say, half he spoke.
The other portion, as he shaped it thus
For argumentatory purposes,
He felt his foe was foolish to dispute.
Some arbitrary accidental thoughts
That crossed his mind, amusing because new,
He chose to represent as fixtures there,
Invariable convictions (such they seemed
Beside his interlocutor's loose cards
Flung daily down, and not the same way twice)
While certain hell-deep instincts, man's weak tongue
Is never bold to utter in their truth
Because styled hell-deep ('t is an old mistake
To place hell at the bottom of the earth)
He ignored these, — not having in readiness
Their nomenclature and philosophy :
He said true things, but called them by wrong names.
'On the whole,' he thought, 'I justify myself
On every point where cavillers like this
Oppugn my life : he tries one kind of fence,
I close, he's worsted, that's enough for him.
He's on the ground : if ground should break away
I take my stand on, there's a firmer yet
Beneath it, both of us may sink and reach.
His ground was over mine and broke the first :
So, let him sit with me this many a year !'

He did not sit five minutes. Just a week
Sufficed his sudden healthy vehemence.
Something had struck him in the 'Outward-bound'
Another way than Blougram's purpose was :
And having bought, not cabin-furniture
But settler's-implements (enough for three)
And started for Australia — there, I hope,
By this time he has tested his first plough,
And studied his last chapter of St. John.

My Last Duchess

That's my last Duchess painted on the wall,
Looking as if she were alive. I call
That piece a wonder, now: Frà Pandolf's hands
Worked busily a day, and there she stands.
Will't please you sit and look at her? I said
'Frà Pandolf' by design, for never read
Strangers like you that pictured countenance,
The depth and passion of its earnest glance,
But to myself they turned (since none puts by
The curtain I have drawn for you, but I)
And seemed as they would ask me, if they durst,
How such a glance came there; so, not the first
Are you to turn and ask thus. Sir, 't was not
Her husband's presence only, called that spot
Of joy into the Duchess' cheek: perhaps
Frà Pandolf chanced to say 'Her mantle laps
Over my lady's wrist too much,' or 'Paint
Must never hope to reproduce the faint
Half-flush that dies along her throat:' such stuff
Was courtesy, she thought, and cause enough
For calling up that spot of joy. She had
A heart — how shall I say? — too soon made glad,
Too easily impressed; she liked whate'er
She looked on, and her looks went everywhere.
Sir, 't was all one! My favour at her breast,
The dropping of the daylight in the West,
The bough of cherries some officious fool
Broke in the orchard for her, the white mule
She rode with round the terrace — all and each
Would draw from her alike the approving speech,
Or blush, at least. She thanked men, — good! but thanked
Somehow — I know not how — as if she ranked
My gift of a nine-hundred-years-old name
With anybody's gift. Who'd stoop to blame

This sort of trifling? Even had you skill
In speech — (which I have not) — to make your will
Quite clear to such an one, and say, 'Just this
Or that in you disgust me; here you miss,
Or there exceed the mark' — and if she let
Herself be lessoned so, nor plainly set
Her wits to yours, forsooth, and made excuse,
— E'en then would be some stooping; and I choose
Never to stoop. Oh sir, she smiled, no doubt,
Whene'er I passed her; but who passed without
Much the same smile? This grew; I gave commands
Then all smiles stopped together. There she stands
As if alive. Will't please you rise? We'll meet
The company below, then. I repeat,
The Count your master's known munificence
Is ample warrant that no just pretence
Of mine for dowry will be disallowed;
Though his fair daughter's self, as I avowed
At starting, is my object. Nay, we'll go
Together down, sir. Notice Neptune, though,
Taming a sea-horse, thought a rarity,
Which Claus of Innsbruck cast in bronze for me!

Waring

I

I

What's become of Waring
Since he gave us all the slip,
Chose land-travel or seafaring,
Boots and chest or staff and scrip,
Rather than pace up and down
Any longer London town?

II

Who'd have guessed it from his lip
Or his brow's accustomed bearing,
On the night he thus took ship
Or started landward? — little caring
For us, it seems, who supped together
(Friends of his too, I remember)
And walked home thro' the merry weather,
The snowiest in all December.
I left his arm that night myself
For what's-his-name's, the new prose-poet
Who wrote the book there, on the shelf —
How, forsooth, was I to know it
If Waring meant to glide away
Like a ghost at break of day?
Never looked he half so gay!

III

He was prouder than the devil:
How he must have cursed our revel!
Ay and many other meetings,
Indoor visits, outdoor greetings,
As up and down he paced this London,
With no work done, but great works undone,
Where scarce twenty knew his name.

Why not, then, have earlier spoken,
Written, bustled? Who's to blame
If your silence kept unbroken?
'True, but there were sundry jottings,
Stray-leaves, fragments, blurrs and blottings,
Certain first steps were achieved
Already which' — (is that your meaning?)
'Had well borne out whoe'er believed
In more to come !' But who goes gleaning
Hedgeside chance-blades, while full-sheaved
Stand cornfields by him? Pride, o'erweening
Pride alone, puts forth such claims
O'er the day's distinguished names.

IV

Meantime, how much I loved him,
I find out now I've lost him.
I who cared not if I moved him,
Who could so carelessly accost him,
Henceforth never shall get free
Of his ghostly company,
His eyes that just a little wink
As deep I go into the merit
Of this and that distinguished spirit —
His cheeks' raised colour, soon to sink,
As long I dwell on some stupendous
And tremendous (Heaven defend us !)
Monstr'-inform'-ingens-horrend-ous
Demoniaco-seraphic
Penman's latest piece of graphic.
Nay, my very wrist grows warm
With his dragging weight of arm.
E'en so, swimmingly appears,
Through one's after-supper musings,
Some lost lady of old years
With her beauteous vain endeavour
And goodness unrepaid as ever;
The face, accustomed to refusings,

We, puppies that we were . . . Oh never
Surely, nice of conscience, scrupled
Being aught like false, forsooth, to?
Telling aught but honest truth to?
What a sin, had we centupled
Its possessor's grace and sweetness!
No! she heard in its completeness
Truth, for truth's a weighty matter,
And truth, at issue, we can't flatter!
Well, 't is done with; she's exempt
From damning us thro' such a sally;
And so she glides, as down a valley,
Taking up with her contempt,
Past our reach; and in, the flowers
Shut her unregarded hours.

V

Oh, could I have him back once more,
This Waring, but one half-day more!
Back, with the quiet face of yore,
So hungry for acknowledgment
Like mine! I'd fool him to his bent.
Feed, should not he, to heart's content?
I'd say, 'to only have conceived,
Planned your great works, apart from progress,
Surpasses little works achieved?'
I'd lie so, I should be believed.
I'd make such havoc of the claims
Of the day's distinguished names
To feast him with, as feasts an ogress
Her feverish sharp-toothed gold-crowned child!
Or as one feasts a creature rarely
Captured here, unreconciled
To capture; and completely gives
Its pettish humours license, barely
Requiring that it lives.

VI

Ichabod, Ichabod,
The glory is departed!
Travels Waring East away?
Who, of knowledge, by hearsay,
Reports a man upstarted
Somewhere as a god,
Hordes grown European-hearted,
Millions of the wild made tame
On a sudden at his fame?
In Vishnu-land what Avatar?
Or who in Moscow, toward the Czar,
With the demurest of footfalls
Over the Kremlin's pavement bright
With serpentine and syenite,
Steps, with five other Generals
That simultaneously take snuff,
For each to have pretext enough
And kerchiefwise unfold his sash
Which, softness' self, is yet the stuff
To hold fast where a steel chain snaps,
And leave the grand white neck no gash?
Waring in Moscow, to those rough
Cold northern natures born perhaps,
Like the lambwhite maiden dear
From the circle of mute kings
Unable to repress the tear,
Each as his sceptre down he flings,
To Dian's fane at Taurica,
Where now a captive priestess, she alway
Mingles her tender grave Hellenic speech
With theirs, tuned to the hailstone-beaten beach
As pours some pigeon, from the myrrhy lands
Rapt by the whirlblast to fierce Scythian strands
Where breed the swallows, her melodious cry
Amid their barbarous twitter!
In Russia? Never! Spain were fitter!
Ay, most likely 't is in Spain

That we and Waring meet again
Now, while he turns down that cool narrow lane
Into the blackness, out of grave Madrid
All fire and shine, abrupt as when there's slid
Its stiff gold blazing pall
From some black coffin-lid.
Or, best of all,
I love to think
The leaving us was just a feint;
Back here to London did he slink,
And now works on without a wink
Of sleep, and we are on the brink
Of something great in fresco-paint:
Some garret's ceiling, walls and floor,
Up and down and o'er and o'er
He splashes, as none splashed before
Since great Caldara Polidore.
Or Music means this land of ours
Some favour yet, to pity won
By Purcell from his Rosy Bowers, —
'Give me my so-long promised son,
Let Waring end what I begun!'
Then down he creeps and out he steals
Only when the night conceals
His face; in Kent 't is cherry-time,
Or hops are picking: or at prime
Of March he wanders as, too happy,
Years ago when he was young,
Some mild eve when woods grew sappy
And the early moths had sprung
To life from many a trembling sheath
Woven the warm boughs beneath;
While small birds said to themselves
What should soon be actual song,
And young gnats, by tens and twelves,
Made as if they were the throng
That crowd around and carry aloft
The sound they have nursed, so sweet and pure,

Out of a myriad noises soft,
Into a tone that can endure
Amid the noise of a July noon
When all God's creatures crave their boon,
All at once and all in tune,
And get it, happy as Waring then,
Having first within his ken
What a man might do with men:
And far too glad, in the even-glow,
To mix with the world he meant to take
Into his hand, he told you, so —
And out of it his world to make,
To contract and to expand
As he shut or oped his hand.
Oh Waring, what's to really be?
A clear stage and a crowd to see!
Some Garrick, say, out shall not he
The heart of Hamlet's mystery pluck?
Or, where most unclean beasts are rife,
Some Junius — am I right? — shall tuck
His sleeve, and forth with flaying-knife!
Some Chatterton shall have the luck
Of calling Rowley into life!
Some one shall somehow run a muck
With this old world for want of strife
Sound asleep. Contrive, contrive
To rouse us, Waring! Who's alive?
Our men scarce seem in earnest now.
Distinguished names! — but 't is, somehow,
As if they played at being names
Still more distinguished, like the games
Of children. Turn our sport to earnest
With a visage of the sternest!
Bring the real times back, confessed
Still better than our very best!

I

'When I last saw Waring ...'
(How all turned to him who spoke!
You saw Waring? Truth or joke?
In land-travel or sea-faring?)

II

'We were sailing by Triest
Where a day or two we harboured:
A sunset was in the West,
When, looking over the vessel's side,
One of our company espied
A sudden speck to larboard.
And as a sea-duck flies and swims
At once, so came the light craft up,
With its sole lateen sail that trims
And turns (the water round its rims
Dancing, as round a sinking cup)
And by us like a fish it curled,
And drew itself up close beside,
Its great sail on the instant furled,
And o'er its thwarts a shrill voice cried,
(A neck as bronzed as a Lascar's)
"Buy wine of us, you English Brig?
Or fruit, tobacco and cigars?
A pilot for you to Triest?
Without one, look you ne'er so big,
They'll never let you up the bay!
We natives should know best."
I turned, and "just those fellows' way,"
Our captain said, "The 'long-shore thieves
Are laughing at us in their sleeves." '

III

'In truth, the boy leaned laughing back;
And one, half-hidden by his side

Under the furled sail, soon I spied,
With great grass hat and kerchief black,
Who looked up with his kingly throat,
Said somewhat, while the other shook
His hair back from his eyes to look
Their longest at us; then the boat,
I know not how, turned sharply round,
Laying her whole side on the sea
As a leaping fish does; from the lee
Into the weather, cut somehow
Her sparkling path beneath our bow
And so went off, as with a bound,
Into the rosy and golden half
O' the sky, to overtake the sun
And reach the shore, like the sea-calf
Its singing cave; yet I caught one
Glance ere away the boat quite passed,
And neither time nor toil could mar
Those features: so I saw the last
Of Waring!' — You? Oh, never star
Was lost here but it rose afar!
Look East, where whole new thousands are!
In Vishnu-land what Avatar?

A Light Woman

I

So far as our story approaches the end,
    Which do you pity the most of us three? —
My friend, or the mistress of my friend
    With her wanton eyes, or me?

II

My friend was already too good to lose,
    And seemed in the way of improvement yet,
When she crossed his path with her hunting-noose
    And over him drew her net.

III

When I saw him tangled in her toils,
    A shame, said I, if she adds just him
To her nine-and-ninety other spoils,
    The hundredth for a whim!

IV

And before my friend be wholly hers,
    How easy to prove to him, I said,
An eagle's the game her pride prefers,
    Though she snaps at a wren instead!

V

So, I gave her eyes my own eyes to take,
    My hand sought hers as in earnest need,
And round she turned for my noble sake,
    And gave me herself indeed.

VI

The eagle am I, with my fame in the world,
    The wren is he, with his maiden face.
— You look away and your lip is curled?
    Patience, a moment's space!

VII

For see, my friend goes shaking and white;
    He eyes me as the basilisk:
I have turned, it appears, his day to night,
    Eclipsing his sun's disk.

VIII

And I did it, he thinks, as a very thief:
    'Though I love her — that, he comprehends —
One should master one's passions, (love, in chief)
    And be loyal to one's friends!'

IX

And she, — she lies in my hand as tame
    As a pear late basking over a wall;
Just a touch to try and off it came;
    'T is mine, — can I let it fall?

X

With no mind to eat it, that's the worst!
    Were it thrown in the road, would the case assist?
'T was quenching a dozen blue-flies' thirst
    When I gave its stalk a twist.

XI

And I, — what I seem to my friend, you see:
    What I soon shall seem to his love, you guess:
What I seem to myself, do you ask of me?
    No hero, I confess.

XII

'T is an awkward thing to play with souls,
    And matter enough to save one's own:
Yet think of my friend, and the burning coals
    He played with for bits of stone!

XIII

One likes to show the truth for the truth;
   That the woman was light is very true:
But suppose she says, — Never mind that youth!
   What wrong have I done to you?

XIV

Well, any how, here the story stays,
   So far at least as I understand;
And, Robert Browning, you writer of plays,
   Here's a subject made to your hand!

The Last Ride Together

I

I said — Then, dearest, since 't is so,
Since now at length my fate I know,
Since nothing all my love avails,
Since all, my life seemed meant for, fails,
   Since this was written and needs must be —
My whole heart rises up to bless
Your name in pride and thankfulness!
Take back the hope you gave, — I claim
Only a memory of the same,
— And this beside, if you will not blame,
   Your leave for one more last ride with me.

II

My mistress bent that brow of hers;
Those deep dark eyes where pride demurs
When pity would be softening through,
Fixed me a breathing-while or two
   With life or death in the balance: right!
The blood replenished me again;
My last thought was at least not vain:

79

I and my mistress, side by side
Shall be together, breathe and ride,
So, one day more am I deified.
   Who knows but the world may end to-night?

III

Hush! if you saw some western cloud
All billowy-bosomed, over-bowed
By many benedictions — sun's
And moon's and evening-star's at once —
   And so, you, looking and loving best,
Conscious grew, your passion drew
Cloud, sunset, moonrise, star-shine too,
Down on you, near and yet more near,
Till flesh must fade for heaven was here! —
Thus leant she and lingered — joy and fear!
   Thus lay she a moment on my breast

IV

Then we began to ride. My soul
Smoothed itself out, a long-cramped scroll
Freshening and fluttering in the wind.
Past hopes already lay behind.
   What need to strive with a life awry?
Had I said that, had I done this,
So might I gain, so might I miss.
Might she have loved me? just as well
She might have hated, who can tell!
Where had I been now if the worst befell?
   And here we are riding, she and I.

V

Fail I alone, in words and deeds?
Why, all men strive and who succeeds?
Who rode; it seemed my spirit flew,
Saw other regions, cities new,
   As the world rushed by on either side.

I thought, — All labour, yet no less
Bear up beneath their unsuccess.
Look at the end of work, contrast
The petty done, the undone vast,
This present of theirs with the hopeful past!
   I hoped she would love me; here we ride.

VI

What hand and brain went ever paired?
What heart alike conceived and dared?
What act proved all its thought had been?
What will but felt the fleshly screen?
   We ride and I see her bosom heave.
There's many a crown for who can reach.
Ten lines, a statesman's life in each!
The flag stuck on a heap of bones,
A soldier's doing! what atones?
They scratch his name on the Abbey-stones.
   My riding is better, by their leave.

VII

What does it all mean, poet? Well,
Your brains beat into rhythm, you tell
What we felt only; you expressed
You hold things beautiful the best,
   And pace them in rhyme so, side by side.
'T is something, nay 't is much: but then,
Have you yourself what's best for men?
Are you — poor, sick, old ere your time —
Nearer one whit your own sublime
Than we who never have turned a rhyme?
   Sing, riding's a joy! For me, I ride.

VIII

And you, great sculptor — so, you gave
A score of years to Art, her slave,
And that's your Venus, whence we turn
To yonder girl that fords the burn!
   You acquiesce, and shall I repine?

What, man of music, you grown grey
With notes and nothing else to say,
Is this your sole praise from a friend,
'Greatly his opera's strains intend,
But in music we know how fashions end!'
   I gave my youth; but we ride, in fine.

IX

Who knows what's fit for us? Had fate
Proposed bliss here should sublimate
My being — had I signed the bond —
Still one must lead some life beyond,
   Have a bliss to die with, dim-descried.
This foot once planted on the goal,
This glory-garland round my soul,
Could I descry such? Try and test!
I sink back shuddering from the quest.
Earth being so good, would heaven seem best?
   Now, heaven and she are beyond this ride.

X

And yet — she has not spoke so long!
What if heaven be that, fair and strong
At life's best, with our eyes upturned
Whither life's flower is first discerned,
   We, fixed so, ever should so abide?
What if we still ride on, we two
With life for ever old yet new,
Changed not in kind but in degree,
The instant made eternity, —
And heaven just prove that I and she
   Ride, ride together, for ever ride?

The Heretic's Tragedy

A MIDDLE-AGE INTERLUDE

ROSA MUNDI; SEU, FULCITE ME FLORIBUS. A CONCEIT OF MASTER
GYSBRECHT, CANON-REGULAR OF SAINT JODOCUS-BY-THE-BAR,
YPRES CITY. CANTUQUE, *Virgilius*. AND HATH OFTEN BEEN SUNG
AT HOCK-TIDE AND FESTIVALS. GAVISUS ERAM, *Jessides*.

(It would seem to be a glimpse from the burning of Jacques du
Bourg-Molay, at Paris, A.D. 1314; as distorted by the refraction from
Flemish brain to brain, during the course of a couple of centuries.)

I

PRAEDMONISHETH THE ABBOT DEODAET

The Lord, we look to once for all,
    Is the Lord we should look at, all at once:
He knows not to vary, saith Saint Paul,
    Nor the shadow of turning, for the nonce.
See him no other than as he is!
    Give both the infinitudes their due —
Infinite mercy, but, I wis,
    As infinite a justice too.
                       [*Organ: plagal cadence.*
    As infinite a justice too.

II

ONE-SINGETH

John, Master of the Temple of God,
    Falling to sin the Unknown Sin,
What he bought of Emperor Aldabrod,
    He sold it to Sultan Saladin:
Till, caught by Pope Clement, a-buzzing there,
    Hornet-prince of the mad wasps' hive,
And clipt of his wings in Paris square,
    They bring him now to be burned alive.
           [*And wanteth there grace of lute or clavicithern,*
              ye shall say to confirm him who singeth —
    We bring John now to be burned alive.

In the midst is a goodly gallows built;
    'Twixt fork and fork, a stake is stuck;
But first they set divers tumbrils a-tilt,
    Make a trench all round with the city muck;
Inside they pile log upon log, good store;
    Faggots no few, blocks great and small,
Reach a man's mid-thigh, no less, no more, —
    For they mean he should roast in the sight of all.

CHORUS

We mean he should roast in the sight of all.

IV

Good sappy bavins that kindle forthwith;
    Billets that blaze substantial and slow;
Pine-stump split deftly, dry as pith;
    Larch-heart that chars to a chalk-white glow;
Then up they hoist me John in a chafe,
    Sling him fast like a hog to scorch,
Spit in his face, then leap back safe,
    Sing 'Laudes' and bid clap-to the torch.

CHORUS

Laus Deo — who bids clap-to the torch.

V

John of the Temple, whose fame so bragged,
    Is burning alive in Paris square!
How can he curse, if his mouth is gagged?
    Or wriggle his neck, with a collar there?
Or heave his chest, which a band goes round?
    Or threat with his fist, since his arms are spliced?
Or kick with his feet, now his legs are bound?
    — Thinks John, I will call upon Jesus Christ.
                    [*Here one crosseth himself*

VI

Jesus Christ — John had bought and sold,
    Jesus Christ — John had eaten and drunk;
To him, the Flesh meant silver and gold.
    (*Salvâ reverentiâ.*)
Now it was, 'Saviour, bountiful lamb,
    'I have roasted thee Turks, though men roast me!
See thy servant, the plight wherein I am!
    Art thou a saviour? Save thou me!'

CHORUS

'T is John the mocker cries, 'Save thou me!'

VII

Who maketh God's menace an idle word?
    — Saith, it no more means what it proclaims,
Than a damsel's threat to her wanton bird? —
    For she too prattles of ugly names.
— Saith, he knoweth but one thing, — what he knows?
    That God is good and the rest is breath;
Why else is the same styled Sharon's rose?
    Once a rose, ever a rose, he saith.

CHORUS

O, John shall yet find a rose, he saith!

VIII

Alack, there be roses and roses, John!
    Some, honied of taste like your leman's tongue:
Some, bitter; for why? (roast gaily on!)
    Their tree struck root in devil's-dung.
When Paul once reasoned of righteousness
    And of temperance and of judgment to come,
Good Felix trembled, he could no less:
    John, snickering, crook'd his wicked thumb.

CHORUS

What cometh to John of the wicked thumb?

Ha, ha, John plucketh now at his rose
　　To rid himself of a sorrow at heart!
Lo, — petal on petal, fierce rays unclose;
　　Anther on anther, sharp spikes outstart;
And with blood for dew, the bosom boils;
　　And a gust of sulphur is all its smell;
And lo, he is horribly in the toils
　　Of a coal-black giant flower of hell!

CHORUS

What maketh heaven, That maketh hell.

X

So, as John called now, through the fire amain,
　　On the Name, he had cursed with, all his life —
To the Person, he bought and sold again —
　　For the Face, with his daily buffets rife —
Feature by feature It took its place:
　　And his voice, like a mad dog's choking bark,
At the steady whole of the Judge's face —
　　Died. Forth John's soul flared into the dark.

SUBJOINETH THE ABBOT DEODAET

God help all poor souls lost in the dark!

Holy-Cross Day

ON WHICH THE JEWS WERE FORCED TO ATTEND AN ANNUAL CHRISTIAN SERMON IN ROME

['Now was come about Holy-Cross Day, and now must my lord preach his first sermon to the Jews: as it was of old cared for in the merciful bowels of the Church, that, so to speak, a crumb at least from her conspicuous table here in Rome should be, though but once yearly, cast to the famishing dogs, under-trampled and bespitten-upon beneath the feet of the guests. And a moving sight in truth, this, of so many of the besotted blind restif and ready-to-perish Hebrews! now maternally brought — nay (for He saith, "Compel them to come in") haled, as it were, by the head and hair, and against their obstinate hearts, to partake of the heavenly grace. What awakening, what striving with tears, what working of a yeasty conscience! Nor was my lord wanting to himself on so apt an occasion; witness the abundance of conversions which did incontinently reward him: though not to my lord be altogether the glory.' — *Diary by the Bishop's Secretary*, 1600.]

What the Jews really said, on thus being driven to church, was rather to this effect:

I

Fee, faw, fum! bubble and squeak!
Blessedest Thursday's the fat of the week.
Rumble and tumble, sleek and rough,
Stinking and savoury, smug and gruff,
Take the church-road, for the bell's due chime
Gives us the summons — 't is sermon-time!

II

Boh, here's Barnabas! Job, that's you?
Up stumps Solomon — bustling too?
Shame, man! greedy beyond your years
To handsel the bishop's shaving-shears?
Fair play's a jewel! Leave friends in the lurch?
Stand on a line ere you start for the church!

III

Higgledy piggledy, packed we lie,
Rats in a hamper, swine in a stye,
Wasps in a bottle, frogs in a sieve,
Worms in a carcase, fleas in a sleeve.
Hist! square shoulders, settle your thumbs
And buzz for the bishop — here he comes.

IV

Bow, wow, wow — a bone for the dog!
I liken his Grace to an acorned hog.
What, a boy at his side, with the bloom of a lass,
To help and handle my lord's hour-glass!
Didst ever behold so lithe a chine?
His cheek hath laps like a fresh-singed swine.

V

Aaron's asleep — shove hip to haunch,
Or somebody deal him a dig in the paunch!
Look at the purse with the tassel and knob,
And the gown with the angel and thingumbob!
What's he at, quotha? reading his text!
Now you've his curtsey — and what comes next

VI

See to our converts — you doomed black dozen —
No stealing away — nor cog nor cozen!
You five, that were thieves, deserve it fairly;
You seven, that were beggars, will live less sparely;
You took your turn and dipped in the hat,
Got fortune — and fortune gets you; mind that!

VII

Give your first groan — compunction's at work;
And soft! from a Jew you mount to a Turk.
Lo, Micah, — the selfsame beard on chin
He was four times already converted in!
Here's a knife, clip quick — it's a sign of grace —
Or he ruins us all with his hanging-face.

VIII

Whom now is the bishop a-leering at?
I know a point where his text falls pat.
I'll tell him to-morrow, a word just now
Went to my heart and made me vow
I meddle no more with the worst of trades —
Let somebody else pay his serenades.

IX

Groan all together now, whee — hee — hee!
It's a-work, it's a-work, ah, woe is me!
It began, when a herd of us, picked and placed,
Were spurred through the Corso, stripped to the waist;
Jew brutes, with sweat and blood well spent
To usher in worthily Christian Lent.

X

It grew, when the hangman entered our bounds,
Yelled, pricked us out to his church like hounds:
It got to a pitch, when the hand indeed
Which gutted my purse would throttle my creed:
And it overflows when, to even the odd,
Men I helped to their sins help me to their God.

XI

But now, while the scapegoats leave our flock,
And the rest sit silent and count the clock,
Since forced to muse the appointed time
On these precious facts and truths sublime, —
Let us fitly employ it, under our breath,
In saying Ben Ezra's Song of Death.

XII

For Rabbi Ben Ezra, the night he died,
Called sons and sons' sons to his side,
And spoke, 'This world has been harsh and strange;
Something is wrong: there needeth a change.
But what, or where? at the last or first?
In one point only we sinned, at worst.'

XIII

'The Lord will have mercy on Jacob yet,
And again in his border see Israel set.
When Judah beholds Jerusalem,
The stranger-seed shall be joined to them:
To Jacob's House shall the Gentiles cleave.
So the Prophet saith and his sons believe.'

XIV

'Ay, the children of the chosen race
Shall carry and bring them to their place:
In the land of the Lord shall lead the same,
Bondsmen and handmaids. Who shall blame,
When the slaves enslave, the oppressed ones o'er
The oppressor triumph for evermore?'

XV

'God spoke, and gave us the word to keep,
Bade never fold the hands nor sleep
'Mid a faithless world, — at watch and ward,
Till Christ at the end relieve our guard.
By His servant Moses the watch was set:
Though near upon cock-crow, we keep it yet.'

XVI

'Thou! if thou wast He, who at mid-watch came,
By the starlight, naming a dubious name!
And if, too heavy with sleep — too rash
With fear — O Thou, if that martyr-gash
Fell on Thee coming to take thine own,
And we gave the Cross, when we owed the Throne —'

XVII

'Thou art the Judge. We are bruised thus.
But, the Judgment over, join sides with us!
Thine too is the cause! and not more thine
Than ours, is the work of these dogs and swine,
Whose life laughs through and spits at their creed!
Who maintain Thee in word, and defy Thee in deed!'

XVIII

'We withstood Christ then? Be mindful how
At least we withstand Barabbas now!
Was our outrage sore? But the worst we spared,
To have called these — Christians, had we dared!
Let defiance to them pay mistrust of Thee,
And Rome make amends for Calvary!'

XIX

'By the torture, prolonged from age to age,
By the infamy, Israel's heritage,
By the Ghetto's plague, by the garb's disgrace,
By the badge of shame, by the felon's place,
By the branding-tool, the bloody whip,
And the summons to Christian fellowship, —'

XX

'We boast our proof that at least the Jew
Would wrest Christ's name from the Devil's crew.
Thy face took never so deep a shade
But we fought them in it, God our aid!
A trophy to bear, as we march, thy band,
South, East, and on to the Pleasant Land!'

> [*Pope Gregory XVI. abolished this bad business
> of the Sermon.* — R. B.]

Protus

Among these latter busts we count by scores,
Half-emperors and quarter-emperors,
Each with his bay-leaf fillet, loose-thonged vest,
Loric and low-browed Gorgon on the breast, —
One loves a baby face, with violets there,
Violets instead of laurel in the hair,
As those were all the little locks could bear.

Now read here. 'Protus ends a period
Of empery beginning with a god;
Born in the porphyry chamber at Byzant,
Queens by his cradle, proud and ministrant:
And if he quickened breath there, 't would like fire
Pantingly through the dim vast realm transpire.
A fame that he was missing spread afar:
The world from its four corners, rose in war,
Till he was borne out on a balcony
To pacify the world when it should see.
The captains ranged before him, one, his hand
Made baby points at, gained the chief command.
And day by day more beautiful he grew
In shape, all said, in feature and in hue,
While young Greek sculptors, gazing on the child,
Became with old Greek sculpture reconciled.
Already sages laboured to condense
In easy tomes a life's experience:
And artists took grave counsel to impart
In one breath and one hand-sweep, all their art —
To make his graces prompt as blossoming
Of plentifully-watered palms in spring:
Since well beseems it, whoso mounts the throne,
For beauty, knowledge, strength, should stand alone,
And mortals love the letters of his name.'

— Stop! Have you turned two pages? Still the same.
New reign, same date. The scribe goes on to say
How that same year, on such a month and day,
'John the Pannonian, groundedly believed
A blacksmith's bastard, whose hard hand reprieved
The Empire from its fate the year before, —
Came, had a mind to take the crown, and wore
The same for six years (during which the Huns
Kept off their fingers from us), till his sons
Put something in his liquor' — and so forth.
Then a new reign. Stay — 'Take at its just worth'

(Subjoins an annotator) 'what I give
As hearsay. Some think, John let Protus live
And slip away. 'T is said, he reached man's age
At some blind northern court; made, first a page,
Then tutor to the children; last, of use
About the hunting-stables. I deduce
He wrote the little tract "On worming dogs,"
Whereof the name in sundry catalogues
Is extant yet. A Protus of the race
Is rumoured to have died a monk in Thrace, —
And if the same, he reached senility.'

Here's John the Smith's rough-hammered head. Great eye,
Gross jaw and griped lips do what granite can
To give you the crown-grasper. What a man!

'Childe Roland to the Dark Tower Came'

(See Edgar's song in LEAR)

I

My first thought was, he lied in every word,
    That hoary cripple, with malicious eye
    Askance to watch the working of his lie
On mine, and mouth scarce able to afford
Suppression of the glee, that pursed and scored
    Its edge, at one more victim gained thereby.

II

What else should he be set for, with his staff!
    What, save to waylay with his lies, ensnare
    All travellers who might find him posted there,
And ask the road? I guessed what skull-like laugh
Would break, what crutch 'gin write my epitaph
    For pastime in the dusty thoroughfare,

93

III

If at his counsel I should turn aside
  Into that ominous tract which, all agree,
  Hides the Dark Tower. Yet acquiescingly
I did turn as he pointed: neither pride
Nor hope rekindling at the end descried,
  So much as gladness that some end might be.

IV

For, what with my whole world-wide wandering,
  What with my search drawn out thro' years, my hope
  Dwindled into a ghost not fit to cope
With that obstreperous joy success would bring, —
I hardly tried now to rebuke the spring
  My heart made, finding failure in its scope.

V

As when a sick man very near to death
  Seems dead indeed, and feels begin and end
  The tears and takes the farewell of each friend,
And hears one bid the other go, draw breath
Freelier outside, ('since all is o'er,' he saith,
  'And the blow fallen no grieving can amend;')

VI

While some discuss if near the other graves
  Be room enough for this, and when a day
  Suits best for carrying the corpse away,
With care about the banners, scarves and staves:
And still the man hears all, and only craves
  He may not shame such tender love and stay.

VII

Thus, I had so long suffered in this quest,
  Heard failure prophesied so oft, been writ
  So many times among 'The Band' — to wit,
The knights who to the Dark Tower's search addressed
Their steps — that just to fail as they, seemed best,
  And all the doubt was now — should I be fit?

So, quiet as despair, I turned from him,
　　That hateful cripple, out of his highway
　　Into the path he pointed. All the day
Had been a dreary one at best, and dim
Was settling to its close, yet shot one grim
　　Red leer to see the plain catch its estray.

For mark ! no sooner was I fairly found
　　Pledged to the plain, after a pace or two,
　　Than, pausing to throw backward a last view
O'er the safe road, 't was gone; grey plain all round:
Nothing but plain to the horizon's bound.
　　I might go on; nought else remained to do.

So, on I went. I think I never saw
　　Such starved ignoble nature; nothing throve:
　　For flowers — as well expect a cedar grove !
But cockle, spurge, according to their law
Might propagate their kind, with none to awe,
　　You'd think; a burr had been a treasure-trove.

No ! penury, inertness and grimace,
　　In some strange sort, were the land's portion. 'See
　　Or shut your eyes,' said Nature peevishly,
'It nothing skills: I cannot help my case:
'T is the Last Judgment's fire must cure this place,
　　Calcine its clods and set my prisoners free.'

If there pushed any ragged thistle-stalk
　　Above its mates, the head was chopped; the bents
　　Were jealous else. What made those holes and rents
In the dock's harsh swarth leaves, bruised as to baulk
All hope of greenness? 't is a brute must walk
　　Bashing their life out, with a brute's intents.

As for the grass, it grew as scant as hair
    In leprosy; thin dry blades pricked the mud
    Which underneath looked kneaded up with blood,
One stiff blind horse, his every bone a-stare,
Stood stupefied, however he came there:
    Thrust out past service from the devil's stud!

Alive? he might be dead for aught I know,
    With that gaunt and colloped neck a-strain,
    And shut eyes underneath the rusty mane;
Seldom went such grotesqueness with such woe;
I never saw a brute I hated so;
    He must be wicked to deserve such pain.

I shut my eyes and turned them on my heart.
    As a man calls for wine before he fights,
    I asked one draught of earlier, happier sights,
Ere fitly I could hope to play my part.
Think first, fight afterwards — the soldier's art:
    One taste of the old time sets all to rights.

Not it! I fancied Cuthbert's reddening face
    Beneath its garniture of curly gold,
    Dear fellow, till I almost felt him fold
An arm in mine to fix me to the place,
That way he used. Alas, one night's disgrace!
    Out went my heart's new fire and left it cold.

Giles then, the soul of honour — there he stands
    Frank as ten years ago when knighted first.
    What honest man should dare (he said) he durst.
Good — but the scene shifts — faugh! what hangman-hands
Pin to his breast a parchment? His own bands
    Read it. Poor traitor, spit upon and curst!

Better this present than a past like that;
   Back therefore to my darkening path again!
   No sound, no sight as far as eye could strain.
Will the night send a howlet or a bat?
I asked: when something on the dismal flat
   Came to arrest my thoughts and change their train

XIX

A sudden little river crossed my path
   As unexpected as a serpent comes.
   No sluggish tide congenial to the glooms;
This, as it frothed by, might have been a bath
For the fiend's glowing hoof — to see the wrath
   Of its black eddy bespate with flakes and spumes.

XX

So petty yet so spiteful! All along,
   Low scrubby alders kneeled down over it;
   Drenched willows flung them headlong in a fit
Of mute despair, a suicidal throng:
The river which had done them all the wrong,
   Whate'er that was, rolled by, deterred no whit.

XXI

Which, while I forded, — good saints, how I feared
   To set my foot upon a dead man's cheek,
   Each step, or feel the spear I thrust to seek
For hollows, tangled in his hair or beard!
— It may have been a water-rat I speared,
   But, ugh! it sounded like a baby's shriek.

XXII

Glad was I when I reached the other bank.
   Now for a better country. Vain presage!
   Who were the strugglers, what war did they wage,
Whose savage trample thus could pad the dank
Soil to a plash? Toads in a poisoned tank,
   Or wild cats in a red-hot iron cage —

XXIII

The fight must so have seemed in that fell cirque.
  What penned them there, with all the plain to choose?
  No foot-print leading to that horrid mews,
None out of it. Mad brewage set to work
Their brains, no doubt, like galley-slaves the Turk
  Pits for his pastime, Christians against Jews.

XXIV

And more than that — a furlong on — why, there!
  What bad use was that engine for, that wheel,
  Or brake, not wheel — that harrow fit to reel
Men's bodies out like silk? with all the air
Of Tophet's tool, on earth left unaware,
  Or brought to sharpen its rusty teeth of steel.

XXV

Then came a bit of stubbed ground, once a wood,
  Next a marsh, it would seem, and now mere earth
  Desperate and done with; (so a fool finds mirth,
Makes a thing and then mars it, till his mood
Changes and off he goes!) within a rood —
  Bog, clay and rubble, sand and stark black dearth.

XXVI

Now blotches rankling, coloured gay and grim,
  Now patches where some leanness of the soil's
  Broke into moss or substances like boils;
Then came some palsied oak, a cleft in him
Like a distorted mouth that splits its rim
  Gaping at death, and dies while it recoils.

XXVII

And just as far as ever from the end!
  Nought in the distance but the evening, nought
  To point my footstep further! At the thought,
A great black bird, Apollyon's bosom-friend,
Sailed past, nor beat his wide wing dragon-penned
  That brushed my cap — perchance the guide I sought.

XXVIII

For, looking up, aware I somehow grew,
  'Spite of the dusk, the plain had given place
  All round to mountains — with such name to grace
Mere ugly heights and heaps now stolen in view.
How thus they had surprised me, — solve it, you!
  How to get from them was no clearer case.

XXIX

Yet half I seemed to recognize some trick
  Of mischief happened to me, God knows when —
  In a bad dream perhaps. Here ended, then,
Progress this way. When, in the very nick
Of giving up, one time more, came a click
  As when a trap shuts — you're inside the den!

XXX

Burningly it came on me all at once,
  This was the place! those two hills on the right,
  Crouched like two bulls locked horn in horn in fight;
While to the left, a tall scalped mountain . . . Dunce,
Dotard, a-dozing at the very nonce,
  After a life spent training for the sight!

XXXI

What in the midst lay but the Tower itself?
  The round squat turret, blind as the fool's heart,
  Built of brown stone, without a counterpart
In the whole world. The tempest's mocking elf
Points to the shipman thus the unseen shelf
  He strikes on, only when the timbers start.

XXXII

Not see? because of night perhaps? — why, day
  Came back again for that! before it left,
  The dying sunset kindled through a cleft:
The hills, like giants at a hunting, lay,
Chin upon hand, to see the game at bay, —
  'Now stab and end the creature — to the heft!

XXXIII

Not hear? when noise was everywhere ! it tolled
   Increasing like a bell. Names in my ears
   Of all the lost adventurers my peers, —
How such a one was strong, and such was bold,
And such was fortunate, yet each of old
   Lost, lost ! one moment knelled the woe of years.

XXXIV

There they stood, ranged along the hill-sides, met
   To view the last of me, a living frame
   For one more picture ! in a sheet of flame
I saw them and I knew them all. And yet
Dauntless the slug-horn to my lips I set,
   And blew. '*Childe Roland to the Dark Tower came.*'

Garden Fancies

II. SIBRANDUS SCHAFNABURGENSIS

I

Plague take all your pedants, say I!
   He who wrote what I hold in my hand,
Centuries back was so good as to die,
   Leaving this rubbish to cumber the land;
This, that was a book in its time,
   Printed on paper and bound in leather,
Last month in the white of a matin-prime
   Just when the birds sang all together.

II

Into the garden I brought it to read,
   And under the arbute and laurustine
Read it, so help me grace in my need,
   From title-page to closing line.
Chapter on chapter did I count,
   As a curious traveller counts Stonehenge;
Added up the mortal amount;
   And then proceeded to my revenge.

III

Yonder's a plum-tree with a crevice
   An owl would build in, were he but sage;
For a lap of moss, like a fine pont-levis
   In a castle of the Middle Age,
Joins to a lip of gum, pure amber;
   When he'd be private, there might he spend
Hours alone in his lady's chamber:
   Into this crevice I dropped our friend.

IV

Splash, went he, as under he ducked,
— At the bottom, I knew, rain-drippings stagnate:
Next, a handful of blossoms I plucked
To bury him with, my bookshelf's magnate;
Then I went in-doors, brought out a loaf,
Half a cheese, and a bottle of Chablis;
Lay on the grass and forgot the oaf
Over a jolly chapter of Rabelais.

V

Now, this morning, betwixt the moss
And gum that locked our friend in limbo,
A spider had spun his web across,
And sat in the midst with arms akimbo:
So, I took pity, for learning's sake,
And, *de profundis, accentibus lætis*,
Cantata! quoth I, as I got a rake;
And up I fished his delectable treatise.

VI

Here you have it, dry in the sun,
With all the binding all of a blister,
And great blue spots where the ink has run,
And reddish streaks that wink and glister
O'er the page so beautifully yellow:
Oh, well have the droppings played their tricks!
Did he guess how toadstools grow, this fellow?
Here's one stuck in his chapter six!

VII

How did he like it when the live creatures
Tickled and toused and browsed him all over,
And worm, slug, eft, with serious features,
Came in, each one, for his right of trover?

— When the water-beetle with great blind deaf face
    Made of her eggs the stately deposit,
And the newt borrowed just so much of the preface
    As tiled in the top of his black wife's closet?

VIII

All that life and fun and romping,
    All that frisking and twisting and coupling,
While slowly our poor friend's leaves were swamping
    And clasps were cracking and covers suppling!
As if you had carried sour John Knox
    To the play-house at Paris, Vienna or Munich,
Fastened him into a front-row box,
    And danced off the ballet with trousers and tunic.

IX

Come, old martyr! What, torment enough is it?
    Back to my room shall you take your sweet self.
Good-bye, mother-beetle; husband-eft, *sufficit!*
    See the snug niche I have made on my shelf!
A.'s book shall prop you up, B.'s shall cover you,
    Here's C. to be grave with, or D. to be gay,
And with E. on each side, and F. right over you,
    Dry-rot at ease till the Judgment-day!

Soliloquy of the Spanish Cloister

I

Gr-r-r — there go, my heart's abhorrence!
  Water your damned flower-pots, do!
If hate killed men, Brother Lawrence,
  God's blood, would not mine kill you!
What? your myrtle-bush wants trimming?
  Oh, that rose has prior claims —
Needs its leaden vase filled brimming?
  Hell dry you up with its flames!

II

At the meal we sit together:
  Salve tibi! I must hear
Wise talk of the kind of weather,
  Sort of season, time of year:
Not a plenteous cork-crop: scarcely
  Dare we hope oak-galls, I doubt:
What's the Latin name for 'parsley'?
  What's the Greek name for Swine's Snout?

III

Whew! We'll have our platter burnished,
  Laid with care on our own shelf!
With a fire-new spoon we're furnished,
  And a goblet for ourself,
Rinsed like something sacrificial
  Ere 't is fit to touch our chaps —
Marked with L. for our initial!
  (He-he! There his lily snaps!)

IV

Saint, forsooth! While brown Dolores
  Squats outside the Convent bank
With Sanchicha, telling stories,
  Steeping tresses in the tank,

Blue-black, lustrous, thick like horsehairs,
  — Can't I see his dead eye glow,
Bright as 't were a Barbary corsair's?
  (That is, if he'd let it show!)

V

When he finishes refection,
  Knife and fork he never lays
Cross-wise, to my recollection,
  As do I, in Jesu's praise.
I the Trinity illustrate,
  Drinking watered orange-pulp —
In three sips the Arian frustrate;
  While he drains his at one gulp.

VI

Oh, those melons? If he's able
  We're to have a feast! so nice!
One goes to the Abbot's table,
  All of us get each a slice.
How go on your flowers? None double?
  Not one fruit-sort can you spy?
Strange! — And I, too, at such trouble,
  Keep them close-nipped on the sly!

VII

There's a great text in Galatians,
  Once you trip on it, entails
Twenty-nine distinct damnations,
  One sure, if another fails:
If I trip him just a-dying,
  Sure of heaven as sure can be,
Spin him round and send him flying
  Off to hell, a Manichee?

105

VIII

Or, my scrofulous French novel
    On grey paper with blunt type!
Simply glance at it, you grovel
    Hand and foot in Belial's gripe:
If I double down its pages
    At the woeful sixteenth print,
When he gathers his greengages,
    Ope a sieve and slip it in 't?

IX

Or, there's Satan! — one might venture
    Pledge one's soul to him, yet leave
Such a flaw in the indenture
    As he'd miss till, past retrieve,
Blasted lay that rose-acacia
    We're so proud of! *Hy, Zy, Hine* ...
'St, there's Vespers! *Plena gratiâ*
    Ave, Virgo! Gr-r-r — you swine!

Meeting at Night

I

The grey sea and the long black land;
And the yellow half-moon large and low;
And the startled little waves that leap
In fiery ringlets from their sleep,
As I gain the cove with pushing prow,
And quench its speed i' the slushy sand.

II

Then a mile of warm sea-scented beach;
Three fields to cross till a farm appears;
A tap at the pane, the quick sharp scratch
And blue spurt of a lighted match,
And a voice less loud, thro' its joys and fears,
Than the two hearts beating each to each!

Parting at Morning

Round the cape of a sudden came the sea,
And the sun looked over the mountain's rim:
And straight was a path of gold for him,
And the need of a world of men for me.

A Woman's Last Word

I

Let's contend no more, Love,
   Strive nor weep:
All be as before, Love,
   — Only sleep!

II

What so wild as words are?
   I and thou
In debate, as birds are,
   Hawk on bough!

III

See the creature stalking
   While we speak!
Hush and hide the talking,
   Cheek on chéek!

IV

What so false as truth is,
   False to thee?
Where the serpent's tooth is
   Shun the tree —

107

V

Where the apple reddens
   Never pry —
Lest we lose our Edens,
   Eve and I.

VI

Be a god and hold me
   With a charm!
Be a man and fold me
   With thine arm!

VII

Teach me, only teach, Love!
   As I ought
I will speak thy speech, Love,
   Think thy thought —

VIII

Meet, if thou require it,
   Both demands,
Laying flesh and spirit
   In thy hands.

IX

That shall be to-morrow
   Not to-night:
I must bury sorrow
   Out of sight:

X

— Must a little weep, Love
   (Foolish me!)
And so fall asleep, Love,
   Loved by thee.

Up at a Villa — Down in the City

AS DISTINGUISHED BY AN ITALIAN PERSON
OF QUALITY

I

Had I but plenty of money, money enough and to spare,
The house for me, no doubt, were a house in the city-square;
Ah, such a life, such a life, as one leads at the window there!

II

Something to see, by Bacchus, something to hear, at least!
There, the whole day long, one's life is a perfect feast;
While up at a villa one lives, I maintain it, no more than a beast.

III

Well now, look at our villa! stuck like the horn of a bull
Just on a mountain-edge as bare as the creature's skull,
Save a mere shag of a bush with hardly a leaf to pull!
— I scratch my own, sometimes, to see if the hair's turned wool.

IV

But the city, oh the city — the square with the houses! Why?
They are stone-faced, white as a curd, there's something to take the
    eye!
Houses in four straight lines, not a single front awry;
You watch who crosses and gossips, who saunters, who hurries by;
Green blinds, as a matter of course, to draw when the sun gets high;
And the shops with fanciful signs which are painted properly.

V

What of a villa? Though winter be over in March by rights,
'T is May perhaps ere the snow shall have withered well off the
    heights:
You've the brown ploughed land before, where the oxen steam and
    wheeze,
And the hills over-smoked behind by the faint grey olive-trees.

VI

Is it better in May, I ask you? You've summer all at once;
In a day he leaps complete with a few strong April suns.
'Mid the sharp short emerald wheat, scarce risen three fingers well,
The wild tulip, at end of its tube, blows out its great red bell
Like a thin clear bubble of blood, for the children to pick and sell.

VII

Is it ever hot in the square? There's a fountain to spout and splash!
In the shade it sings and springs; in the shine such foam-bows
  flash
On the horses with curling fish-tails, that prance and paddle and
  pash
Round the lady atop in her conch — fifty gazers do not abash,
Though all that she wears is some weeds round her waist in a sort
  of sash.

VIII

All the year long at the villa, nothing to see though you linger,
Except yon cypress that points like death's lean lifted forefinger.
Some think fireflies pretty, when they mix i' the corn and mingle,
Or thrid the stinking hemp till the stalks of it seem a-tingle.
Late August or early September, the stunning cicala is shrill,
And the bees keep their tiresome whine round the resinous firs on
  the hill.
Enough of the seasons, — I spare you the months of the fever and
  chill.

IX

Ere you open your eyes in the city, the blessed church-bells begin:
No sooner the bells leave off than the diligence rattles in:
You get the pick of the news, and it costs you never a pin.
By-and-by there's the travelling doctor gives pills, lets blood, draws
  teeth;
Or the Pulcinello-trumpet breaks up the market beneath.
At the post-office such a scene-picture — the new play, piping hot!
And a notice how, only this morning, three liberal thieves were
  shot.

Above it, behold the Archbishop's most fatherly of rebukes,
And beneath, with his crown and his lion, some little new law of
the Duke's!
Or a sonnet with flowery marge, to the Reverend Don So-and-so
Who is Dante, Boccaccio, Petrarca, Saint Jerome and Cicero,
'And moreover,' (the sonnet goes rhyming), 'the skirts of Saint
Paul has reached,
Having preached us those six Lent-lectures more unctuous than
ever he preached.'
Noon strikes, — here sweeps the procession! our Lady borne
smiling and smart
With a pink gauze gown all spangles, and seven swords stuck in
her heart!
Bang-whang-whang goes the drum, *tootle-te-tootle* the fife;
No keeping one's haunches still: it's the greatest pleasure in life.

X

But bless you, it's dear — it's dear! fowls, wine, at double the rate.
They have clapped a new tax upon salt, and what oil pays passing
the gate
It's a horror to think of. And so, the villa for me, not the city!
Beggars can scarcely be choosers: but still — ah, the pity, the pity!
Look, two and two go the priests, then the monks with cowls and
sandals,
And the penitents dressed in white shirts, a-holding the yellow
candles;
One, he carries a flag up straight, and another a cross with handles
And the Duke's guard brings up the rear, for the better prevention
of scandals:
Bang-whang-whang goes the drum, *tootle-te-tootle* the fife.
Oh, a day in the city-square, there is no such pleasure in life!

A Toccata of Galuppi's

I

Oh Galuppi, Baldassaro, this is very sad to find!
I can hardly misconceive you; it would prove me deaf and blind;
But although I take your meaning, 't is with such a heavy mind!

II

Here you come with your old music, and here's all the good it
  brings.
What, they lived once thus at Venice where the merchants were
  the kings,
Where Saint Mark's is, where the Doges used to wed the sea with
  rings?

III

Ay, because the sea's the street there; and 't is arched by . . . what
  you call
. . . Shylock's bridge with houses on it, where they kept the
  carnival:
I was never out of England — it's as if I saw it all.

IV

Did young people take their pleasure when the sea was warm in
  May?
Balls and masks begun at midnight, burning ever to mid-day,
When they made up fresh adventures for the morrow, do you say?

V

Was a lady such a lady, cheeks so round and lips so red, —
On her neck the small face buoyant, like a bell-flower on its bed,
O'er the breast's superb abundance where a man might base his
  head?

VI

Well, and it was graceful of them — they'd break talk off and
  afford
— She, to bite her mask's black velvet — he, to finger on his sword,
While you sat and played Toccatas, stately at the clavichord?

What? Those lesser thirds so plaintive, sixths diminished, sigh on
    sigh,
Told them something? Those suspensions, those solutions —
    'Must we die?'
Those commiserating sevenths — 'Life might last! we can but
    try!'

VIII

'Were you happy?' — 'Yes.' — 'And are you still as happy?' —
    'Yes. And you?'
— 'Then, more kisses!' — 'Did *I* stop them, when a million
    seemed so few?'
Hark, the dominant's persistence till it must be answered to!

IX

So, an octave struck the answer. Oh, they praised you, I dare say!
'Brave Galuppi! that was music! good alike at grave and gay!
I can always leave off talking when I hear a master play!'

X

Then they left you for their pleasure: till in due time, one by one,
Some with lives that came to nothing, some with deeds as well
    undone,
Death stepped tacitly and took them where they never see the sun.

XI

But when I sit down to reason, think to take my stand nor swerve,
While I triumph o'er a secret wrung from nature's close reserve,
In you come with your cold music till I creep thro' every nerve.

XII

Yes, you, like a ghostly cricket, creaking where a house was
    burned:
'Dust and ashes, dead and done with, Venice spent what Venice
    earned.
The soul, doubtless, is immortal — where a soul can be discerned.'

'Yours for instance: you know physics, something of geology,
Mathematics are your pastime; souls shall rise in their degree;
Butterflies may dread extinction, — you'll not die, it cannot be!'

'As for Venice and her people, merely born to bloom and drop,
Here on earth they bore their fruitage, mirth and folly were the
       crop:
What of soul was left, I wonder, when the kissing had to stop?'

'Dust and ashes!' So you creak it, and I want the heart to scold.
Dear dead women, with such hair, too — what's become of all the
       gold
Used to hang and brush their bosoms? I feel chilly and grown old.

My Star

All that I know
   Of a certain star
Is, it can throw
   (Like the angled spar)
Now a dart of red,
   Now a dart of blue;
Till my friends have said
   They would fain see, too,
My star that dartles the red and the blue!
Then it stops like a bird; like a flower, hangs furled:
   They must solace themselves with the Saturn above it.
What matter to me if their star is a world?
   Mine has opened its soul to me; therefore I love it.

Two in the Campagna

I

I wonder do you feel to-day
   As I have felt since, hand in hand,
We sat down on the grass, to stray
   In spirit better through the land,
This morn of Rome and May?

II

For me, I touched a thought, I know,
   Has tantalized me many times,
(Like turns of thread the spiders throw
   Mocking across our path) for rhymes
To catch at and let go.

III

Help me to hold it ! First it left
   The yellowing fennel, run to seed
There, branching from the brickwork's cleft,
   Some old tomb's ruin : yonder weed
Took up the floating weft,

IV

Where one small orange cup amassed
   Five beetles, — blind and green they grope
Among the honey-meal : and last,
   Everywhere on the grassy slope
I traced it. Hold it fast !

V

The champaign with its endless fleece
   Of feathery grasses everywhere !
Silence and passion, joy and peace,
   And everlasting wash of air —
Rome's ghost since her decease.

VI

Such life here, through such lengths of hours,
    Such miracles performed in play,
Such primal naked forms of flowers,
    Such letting nature have her way
While heaven looks from its towers!

VII

How say you? Let us, O my dove,
    Let us be unashamed of soul,
As earth lies bare to heaven above!
    How is it under our control
To love or not to love?

VIII

I would that you were all to me,
    You that are just so much, no more.
Nor yours nor mine, nor slave nor free!
    Where does the fault lie? What the core
O' the wound, since wound must be?

IX

I would I could adopt your will,
    See with your eyes, and set my heart
Beating by yours, and drink my fill
    At your soul's springs, — your part my part
In life, for good and ill.

X

No. I yearn upward, touch you close,
    Then stand away. I kiss your cheek,
Catch your soul's warmth, — I pluck the rose
    And love it more than tongue can speak —
Then the good minute goes.

Already how am I so far
   Out of that minute? Must I go
Still like the thistle-ball, no bar,
   Onward, whenever light winds blow.
Fixed by no friendly star?

XII

Just when I seemed about to learn!
   Where is the thread now? Off again!
The old trick! Only I discern —
   Infinite passion, and the pain
Of finite hearts that yearn.

Love in a Life

I

Room after room,
I hunt the house through
We inhabit together.
Heart, fear nothing, for, heart, thou shalt find her —
Next time, herself! — not the trouble behind her
Left in the curtain, the couch's perfume!
As she brushed it, the cornice-wreath blossomed anew:
Yon looking-glass gleamed at the wave of her feather.

II

Yet the day wears,
And door succeeds door;
I try the fresh fortune —
Range the wide house from the wing to the centre.
Still the same chance! she goes out as I enter.
Spend my whole day in the quest, — who cares?
But 't is twilight, you see, — with such suites to explore,
Such closets to search, such alcoves to importune!

117

Life in a Love

Escape me?
Never —
Beloved!
While I am I, and you are you,
   So long as the world contains us both,
   Me the loving and you the loth,
While the one eludes, must the other pursue.
My life is a fault at last, I fear:
   It seems too much like a fate, indeed!
   Though I do my best I shall scarce succeed.
But what if I fail of my purpose here?
It is but to keep the nerves at strain,
   To dry one's eyes and laugh at a fall,
And, baffled, get up and begin again, —
   So the chace takes up one's life, that's all.
While, look but once from your farthest bound
   At me so deep in the dust and dark,
No sooner the old hope goes to ground
   Than a new one, straight to the self-same mark,
I shape me —
Ever
Removed!

Memorabilia

I

Ah, did you once see Shelley plain,
   And did he stop and speak to you
And did you speak to him again?
   How strange it seems and new!

II

But you were living before that,
   And also you are living after;

And the memory I started at —
　　My starting moves your laughter

III

I crossed a moor, with a name of its own
　　And a certain use in the world no doubt,
Yet a hand's-breadth of it shines alone
　　'Mid the blank miles round about:

IV

For there I picked up on the heather
　　And there I put inside my breast
A moulted feather, an eagle-feather!
　　Well, I forget the rest.

James Lee's Wife

III. IN THE DOORWAY

I

The swallow has set her six young on the rail,
　　And looks sea-ward:
The water's in stripes like a snake, olive-pale
　　To the leeward, —
On the weather-side, black, spotted white with the wind.
'Good fortune departs, and disaster's behind,' —
Hark, the wind with its wants and its infinite wail!

II

Our fig-tree, that leaned for the saltness, has furled
　　Her five fingers,
Each leaf like a hand opened wide to the world
　　Where there lingers
No glint of the gold, Summer sent for her sake:
How the vines writhe in rows, each impaled on its stake!
My heart shrivels up and my spirit shrinks curled.

III

Yet here are we two; we have love, house enough,
  With the field there,
This house of four rooms, that field red and rough,
  Though it yield there,
For the rabbit that robs, scarce a blade or a bent;
If a magpie alight now, it seems an event;
And they both will be gone at November's rebuff.

IV

But why must cold spread? but wherefore bring change
  To the spirit,
God meant should mate his with an infinite range,
  And inherit
His power to put life in the darkness and cold?
Oh, live and love worthily, bear and be bold!
Whom Summer made friends of, let Winter estrange!

VI. READING A BOOK, UNDER THE CLIFF

I

'Still ailing, Wind? Wilt be appeased or no?
  Which needs the other's office, thou or I?
Dost want to be disburthened of a woe,
  And can, in truth, my voice untie
Its links, and let it go?'

II

'Art thou a dumb wronged thing that would be righted,
  Entrusting thus thy cause to me? Forbear!
No tongue can mend such pleadings; faith, requited
  With falsehood, — love, at last aware
Of scorn, — hopes, early blighted, —'

III

'We have them; but I know not any tone
   So fit as thine to falter forth a sorrow:
Dost think men would go mad without a moan,
   If they knew any way to borrow
A pathos like thy own?'

IV

'Which sigh wouldst mock, of all the sighs? The one
   So long escaping from lips starved and blue,
That lasts while on her pallet-bed the nun
   Stretches her length; her foot comes through
The straw she shivers on;'

V

'You had not thought she was so tall: and spent,
   Her shrunk lids open, her lean fingers shut
Close, close, their sharp and livid nails indent
   The clammy palm; then all is mute:
That way, the spirit went.'

VI

'Or wouldst thou rather that I understand
   Thy will to help me? — like the dog I found
Once, pacing sad this solitary strand,
   Who would not take my food, poor hound,
But whined and licked my hand.'

Abt Vogler

AFTER HE HAS BEEN EXTEMPORIZING UPON THE
MUSICAL INSTRUMENT OF HIS INVENTION

I

Would that the structure brave, the manifold music I build,
    Bidding my organ obey, calling its keys to their work,
Claiming each slave of the sound, at a touch, as when Solomon
    willed
    Armies of angels that soar, legions of demons that lurk,
Man, brute, reptile, fly, — alien of end and of aim,
    Adverse, each from the other heaven-high, hell-deep removed, —
Should rush into sight at once as he named the ineffable Name,
    And pile him a palace straight, to pleasure the princess he loved!

II

Would it might tarry like his, the beautiful building of mine,
    This which my keys in a crowd pressed and importuned to raise!
Ah, one and all, how they helped, would dispart now and now
    combine,
    Zealous to hasten the work, heighten their master his praise!
And one would bury his brow with a blind plunge down to hell,
    Burrow awhile and build, broad on the roots of things,
Then up again swim into sight, having based me my palace well,
    Founded it, fearless of flame, flat on the nether springs.

III

And another would mount and march, like the excellent minion
    he was,
    Ay, another and yet another, one crowd but with many a crest,
Raising my rampired walls of gold as transparent as glass,
    Eager to do and die, yield each his place to the rest:
For higher still and higher (as a runner tips with fire,
    When a great illumination surprises a festal night —
Outlining round and round Rome's dome from space to spire)
    Up, the pinnacled glory reached, and the pride of my soul was
    in sight.

IV

In sight? Not half! for it seemed, it was certain, to match man's
    birth,
    Nature in turn conceived, obeying an impulse as I ;
And the emulous heaven yearned down, made effort to reach the
    earth,
    As the earth had done her best, in my passion, to scale the sky :
Novel splendours burst forth, grew familiar and dwelt with mine,
    Not a point nor peak but found and fixed its wandering star ;
Meteor-moons, balls of blaze : and they did not pale nor pine,
    For earth had attained to heaven, there was no more near nor far.

V

Nay more ; for there wanted not who walked in the glare and glow,
    Presences plain in the place ; or, fresh from the Protoplast,
Furnished for ages to come, when a kindlier wind should blow,
    Lured now to begin and live, in a house to their liking at last ;
Or else the wonderful Dead who have passed through the body
    and gone,
    But were back once more to breathe in an old world worth
    their new :
What never had been, was now ; what was, as it shall be anon ;
    And what is, — shall I say, matched both? for I was made
    perfect too.

VI

All through my keys that gave their sounds to a wish of my soul,
    All through my soul that praised as its wish flowed visibly forth,
All through music and me ! For think, had I painted the whole,
    Why, there it had stood, to see, nor the process so wonder-worth :
Had I written the same, made verse — still, effect proceeds from
    cause,
    Ye know why the forms are fair, ye hear how the tale is told ;
It is all triumphant art, but art in obedience to laws,
    Painter and poet are proud in the artist-list enrolled : —

123

VII

But here is the finger of God, a flash of the will that can,
    Existent behind all laws, that made them and, lo, they are!
And I know not if, save in this, such gift be allowed to man,
    That out of three sounds he frame, not a fourth sound, but a star.
Consider it well: each tone of our scale in itself is nought;
    It is everywhere in the world — loud, soft, and all is said:
Give it to me to use! I mix it with two in my thought:
    And, there! Ye have heard and seen: consider and bow the
        head!

VIII

Well, it is gone at last, the palace of music I reared;
    Gone! and the good tears start, the praises that come too slow;
For one is assured at first, one scarce can say that he feared,
    That he even gave it a thought, the gone thing was to go.
Never to be again! But many more of the kind
    As good, nay, better perchance: is this your comfort to me?
To me, who must be saved because I cling with my mind
    To the same, same self, same love, same God: ay, what was,
        shall be.

IX

Therefore to whom turn I but to thee, the ineffable Name?
    Builder and maker, thou, of houses not made with hands!
What, have fear of change from thee who art ever the same?
    Doubt that thy power can fill the heart that thy power expands?
There shall never be one lost good! What was, shall live as before;
    The evil is null, is nought, is silence implying sound;
What was good shall be good, with, for evil, so much good more;
    On the earth the broken arcs; in the heaven, a perfect round.

X

All we have willed or hoped or dreamed of good shall exist;
    Not its semblance, but itself; no beauty, nor good, nor power
Whose voice has gone forth, but each survives for the melodist
    When eternity affirms the conception of an hour.

The high that proved too high, the heroic for earth too hard,
  The passion that left the ground to lose itself in the sky,
Are music sent up to God by the lover and the bard;
  Enough that he heard it once: we shall hear it by-and-by.

XI

And what is our failure here but a triumph's evidence
  For the fulness of the days? Have we withered or agonized?
Why else was the pause prolonged but that singing might issue
    thence?
  Why rushed the discords in but the harmony should be prized?
Sorrow is hard to bear, and doubt is slow to clear,
  Each sufferer says his say, his scheme of the weal and woe:
But God has a few of us whom he whispers in the ear;
  The rest may reason and welcome: 't is we musicians know.

XII

Well, it is earth with me; silence resumes her reign:
  I will be patient and proud, and soberly acquiesce.
Give me the keys. I feel for the common chord again,
  Sliding by semitones, till I sink to the minor, — yes,
And I blunt it into a ninth, and I stand on alien ground,
  Surveying awhile the heights I rolled from into the deep;
Which, hark, I have dared and done, for my resting-place is found,
  The C Major of this life: so, now I will try to sleep.

Caliban upon Setebos; or,
Natural Theology in the Island

'Thou thoughtest that I was altogether such a one as thyself'

['Will sprawl, now that the heat of day is best,
Flat on his belly in the pit's much mire,
With elbows wide, fists clenched to prop his chin.
And, while he kicks both feet in the cool slush,
And feels about his spine small eft-things course,
Run in and out each arm, and make him laugh:
And while above his head a pompion-plant,
Coating the cave-top as a brow its eye,
Creeps down to touch and tickle hair and beard,
And now a flower drops with a bee inside,
And now a fruit to snap at, catch and crunch, —
He looks out o'er yon sea which sunbeams cross
And recross till they weave a spider-web
(Meshes of fire, some great fish breaks at times)
And talks to his own self, howe'er he please,
Touching that other, whom his dam called God.
Because to talk about Him, vexes — ha,
Could He but know! and time to vex is now,
When talk is safer than in winter-time.
Moreover Prosper and Miranda sleep
In confidence he drudges at their task,
And it is good to cheat the pair, and gibe,
Letting the rank tongue blossom into speech.]

Setebos, Setebos, and Setebos!
'Thinketh, He dwelleth i' the cold o' the moon.

'Thinketh He made it, with the sun to match,
But not the stars; the stars came otherwise;
Only made clouds, winds, meteors, such as that:
Also this isle, what lives and grows thereon,
And snaky sea which rounds and ends the same.

'Thinketh, it came of being ill at ease:
He hated that He cannot change His cold,
Nor cure its ache. 'Hath spied an icy fish
That longed to 'scape the rock-stream where she lived,
And thaw herself within the lukewarm brine
O' the lazy sea her stream thrusts far amid,
A crystal spike 'twixt two warm walls of wave;
Only, she ever sickened, found repulse
At the other kind of water, not her life,
(Green-dense and dim-delicious, bred o' the sun)
Flounced back from bliss she was not born to breathe,
And in her old bounds buried her despair,
Hating and loving warmth alike: so He.

'Thinketh, He made thereat the sun, this isle,
Trees and the fowls here, beast and creeping thing.
Yon otter, sleek-wet, black, lithe as a leech;
Yon auk, one fire-eye in a ball of foam,
That floats and feeds; a certain badger brown
He hath watched hunt with that slant white-wedge eye
By moonlight; and the pie with the long tongue
That pricks deep into oakwarts for a worm,
And says a plain word when she finds her prize,
But will not eat the ants; the ants themselves
That build a wall of seeds and settled stalks
About their hole — He made all these and more,
Made all we see, and us, in spite: how else?
He could not, Himself, make a second self
To be His mate; as well have made Himself:
He would not make what he mislikes or slights,
An eyesore to Him, or not worth His pains:
But did, in envy, listlessness or sport,
Make what Himself would fain, in a manner, be —
Weaker in most points, stronger in a few,
Worthy, and yet mere playthings all the while,
Things He admires and mocks too, — that is it.
Because, so brave, so better though they be,
It nothing skills if He begin to plague.

Look now, I melt a gourd-fruit into mash,
Add honeycomb and pods, I have perceived,
Which bite like finches when they bill and kiss, —
Then, when froth rises bladdery, drink up all,
Quick, quick, till maggots scamper through my brain;
Last, throw me on my back i' the seeded thyme,
And wanton, wishing I were born a bird.
Put case, unable to be what I wish,
I yet could make a live bird out of clay:
Would not I take clay, pinch my Caliban
Able to fly? — for, there, see, he hath wings,
And great comb like the hoopoe's to admire,
And there, a sting to do his foes offence,
There, and I will that he begin to live,
Fly to yon rock-top, nip me off the horns
Of grigs high up that make the merry din,
Saucy through their veined wings, and mind me not.
In which feat, if his leg snapped, brittle clay,
And he lay stupid-like, — why, I should laugh;
And if he, spying me, should fall to weep,
Beseech me to be good, repair his wrong,
Bid his poor leg smart less or grow again, —
Well, as the chance were, this might take or else
Not take my fancy: I might hear his cry,
And give the mankin three sound legs for one,
Or pluck the other off, leave him like an egg,
And lessoned he was mine and merely clay.
Were this no pleasure, lying in the thyme,
Drinking the mash, with brain become alive,
Making and marring clay at will? So He.

'Thinketh, such shows nor right nor wrong in Him,
Nor kind, nor cruel: He is strong and Lord.
'Am strong myself compared to yonder crabs
That march now from the mountain to the sea,
'Let twenty pass, and stone the twenty-first,
Loving not, hating not, just choosing so.
'Say, the first straggler that boasts purple spots

Shall join the file, one pincer twisted off;
'Say, this bruised fellow shall receive a worm,
And two worms he whose nippers end in red;
As it likes me each time, I do: so He.

Well then, 'supposeth He is good i' the main,
Placable if His mind and ways were guessed,
But rougher than His handiwork, be sure!
Oh, He hath made things worthier than Himself,
And envieth that, so helped, such things do more
Than He who made them! What consoles but this?
That they, unless through Him, do nought at all,
And must submit: what other use in things?
'Hath cut a pipe of pithless elder joint
That, blown through, gives exact the scream o' the jay
When from her wing you twitch the feathers blue:
Sound this, and little birds that hate the jay
Flock within stone's throw, glad their foe is hurt:
Put case such pipe could prattle and boast forsooth
'I catch the birds, I am the crafty thing,
I make the cry my maker cannot make
With his great round mouth; he must blow through mine!'
Would not I smash it with my foot? So He.

But wherefore rough, why cold and ill at ease?
Aha, that is a question! Ask, for that,
What knows, — the something over Setebos
That made Him, or He, may be, found and fought,
Worsted, drove off and did to nothing, perchance.
There may be something quiet o'er His head,
Out of His reach, that feels nor joy nor grief,
Since both derive from weakness in some way.
I joy because the quails come; would not joy
Could I bring quails here when I have a mind:
This Quiet, all it hath a mind to, doth.
'Esteemeth stars the outposts of its couch,
But never spends much thought nor care that way.
It may look up, work up, — the worse for those

It works on! 'Careth but for Setebos
The many-handed as a cuttle-fish,
Who, making Himself feared through what He does,
Looks up, first, and perceives he cannot soar
To what is quiet and hath happy life;
Next looks down here, and out of very spite
Makes this a bauble-world to ape yon real,
These good things to match those as hips do grapes.
'T is solace making baubles, ay, and sport.
Himself peeped late, eyed Prosper at his books
Careless and lofty, lord now of the isle:
Vexed, 'stitched a book of broad leaves, arrow-shaped,
Wrote thereon, he knows what, prodigious words:
Has peeled a wand and called it by a name;
Weareth at whiles for an enchanter's robe
The eyed skin of a supple oncelot;
And hath an ounce sleeker than youngling mole,
A four-legged serpent he makes cower and couch,
Now snarl, now hold its breath and mind his eye.
And saith she is Miranda and my wife:
'Keeps for his Ariel a tall pouch-bill crane
He bids go wade for fish and straight disgorge;
Also a sea-beast, lumpish, which he snared,
Blinded the eyes of, and brought somewhat tame,
And split its toe-webs, and now pens the drudge
In a hole o' the rock and calls him Caliban;
A bitter heart that bides its time and bites.
'Plays thus at being Prosper in a way,
Taketh his mirth with make-believes: so He.

His dam held that the Quiet made all things
Which Setebos vexed only: 'holds not so.
Who made them weak, meant weakness He might vex,
Had He meant other, while His hand was in,
Why not make horny eyes no thorn could prick,
Or plate my scalp with bone against the snow,
Or overscale my flesh 'neath joint and joint,

Like an orc's armour? Ay, — so spoil His sport!
He is the One now: only He doth all.

'Saith, He may like, perchance, what profits Him.
Ay, himself loves what does him good; but why?
'Gets good no otherwise. This blinded beast
Loves whoso places flesh-meat on his nose,
But, had he eyes, would want no help, but hate
Or love, just as it liked him: He hath eyes.
Also it pleaseth Setebos to work,
Use all His hands, and exercise much craft,
By no means for the love of what is worked.
'Tasteth, himself, no finer good i' the world
When all goes right, in this safe summer-time,
And he wants little, hungers, aches not much,
Than trying what to do with wit and strength.
'Falls to make something: 'piled yon pile of turfs,
And squared and stuck there squares of soft white chalk,
And, with a fish-tooth, scratched a moon on each,
And set up endwise certain spikes of tree,
And crowned the whole with a sloth's skull a-top,
Found dead i' the woods, too hard for one to kill.
No use at all i' the work, for work's sole sake;
'Shall some day knock it down again: so He.

'Saith He is terrible: watch His feats in proof!

One hurricane will spoil six good months' hope.
He hath a spite against me, that I know,
Just as He favours Prosper, who knows why?
So it is, all the same, as well I find.
'Wove wattles half the winter, fenced them firm
With stone and stake to stop she-tortoises
Crawling to lay their eggs here: well, one wave,
Feeling the foot of Him upon its neck,
Gaped as a snake does, lolled out its large tongue,
And licked the whole labour flat: so much for spite.
'Saw a ball flame down late (yonder it lies)
Where, half an hour before, I slept i' the shade:

Often they scatter sparkles: there is force!
'Dug up a newt He may have envied once
And turned to stone, shut up inside a stone.
Please Him and hinder this? — What Prosper does?
Aha, if He would tell me how! Not He!
There is the sport: discover how or die!
All need not die, for of the things o' the isle
Some flee afar, some dive, some run up trees;
Those at His mercy, — why, they please Him most
When .. when .. well, never try the same way twice!
Repeat what act has pleased, He may grow wroth.
You must not know His ways, and play Him off,
Sure of the issue. 'Doth the like himself:
'Spareth a squirrel that it nothing fears
But steals the nut from underneath my thumb,
And when I threat, bites stoutly in defence:
'Spareth an urchin that contrariwise,
Curls up into a ball, pretending death
For fright at my approach: the two ways please.
But what would move my choler more than this,
That either creature counted on its life
To-morrow and next day and all days to come,
Saying, forsooth, in the inmost of its heart,
'Because he did so yesterday with me,
And otherwise with such another brute,
So must he do henceforth and always.' — Ay?
Would teach the reasoning couple what 'must' means!
'Doth as he likes, or wherefore Lord? So He.

'Conceiveth all things will continue thus,
And we shall have to live in fear of Him
So long as He lives, keeps His strength: no change,
If He have done His best, make no new world
To please Him more, so leave off watching this, —
If He surprise not even the Quiet's self
Some strange day, — or, suppose, grow into it
As grubs grow butterflies: else, here are we,
And there is He, and nowhere help at all.

'Believeth with the life, the pain shall stop.
His dam held different, that after death
He both plagued enemies and feasted friends:
Idly! He doth His worst in this our life,
Giving just respite lest we die through pain,
Saving last pain for worst, —with which, an end.
Meanwhile, the best way to escape His ire
Is, not to seem too happy. 'Sees, himself,
Yonder two flies, with purple films and pink,
Bask on the pompion bell above: kills both.
'Sees two black painful beetles roll their ball
On head and tail as if to save their lives:
Moves them the stick away they strive to clear.

Even so, 'would have Him misconceive, suppose
This Caliban strives hard and ails no less,
And always, above all else, envies Him;
Wherefore he mainly dances on dark nights,
Moans in the sun, gets under holes to laugh,
And never speaks his mind save housed as now:
Outside, 'groans, curses. If He caught me here,
O'erheard this speech, and asked 'What chucklest at?'
'Would, to appease Him, cut a finger off,
Or of my three kid yearlings burn the best,
Or let the toothsome apples rot on tree,
Or push my tame beast for the orc to taste:
While myself lit a fire, and made a song
And sung it, '*What I hate, be consecrate*
To celebrate Thee and Thy state, no mate
For Thee; what see for envy in poor me?'
Hoping the while, since evils sometimes mend,
Warts rub away and sores are cured with slime,
That some strange day, will either the Quiet catch
And conquer Setebos, or likelier He
Decrepit may doze, doze, as good as die.
[What, what? A curtain o'er the world at once!
Crickets stop hissing; not a bird — or, yes,
There scuds His raven that has told Him all!

133

It was fool's play, this prattling! Ha! The wind
Shoulders the pillared dust, death's house o' the move,
And fast invading fires begin! White blaze —
A tree's head snaps — and there, there, there, there, there,
His thunder follows! Fool to gibe at Him!
Lo! 'Lieth flat and loveth Setebos!
'Maketh his teeth meet through his upper lip,
Will let those quails fly, will not eat this month
One little mess of whelks, so he may 'scape!]

From *Mr. Sludge, 'The Medium'*

You ask perhaps
Why I should condescend to trick at all
If I know a way without it? This is why!
There's a strange secret sweet self-sacrifice
In any desecration of one's soul
To a worthy end, — isn't it Herodotus
(I wish I could read Latin!) who describes
The single gift o' the land's virginity,
Demanded in those old Egyptian rites,
(I've but a hazy notion — help me, sir!)
For one purpose in the world, one day in a life,
One hour in a day — thereafter, purity,
And a veil thrown o'er the past for evermore!
Well, now, they understood a many things
Down by Nile city, or wherever it was!
I've always vowed, after the minute's lie,
And the end's gain, — truth should be mine henceforth.
This goes to the root o' the matter, sir, — this plain
Plump fact: accept it and unlock with it
The wards of many a puzzle!

Or, finally,
Why should I set so fine a gloss on things?
What need I care? I cheat in self-defence,

And there's my answer to a world of cheats?
Cheat? To be sure, sir! What's the world worth else!
Who takes it as he finds, and thanks his stars?
Don't it want trimming, turning, furbishing up
And polishing over? Your so-styled great men,
Do they accept one truth as truth is found,
Or try their skill at tinkering? What's your world?
Here are you born, who are, I'll say at once,
Of the luckiest kind, whether in head and heart,
Body and soul, or all that helps them both.
Well, now, look back: what faculty of yours
Came to its full, had ample justice done
By growing when rain fell, biding its time,
Solidifying growth when earth was dead,
Spiring up, broadening wide, in seasons due?
Never! You shot up and frost nipped you off,
Settled to sleep when sunshine bade you sprout;
One faculty thwarted its fellow: at the end,
All you boast is 'I had proved a topping tree
In other climes' — yet this was the right clime
Had you foreknown the seasons. Young, you've force
Wasted like well-streams: old, — oh, then indeed,
Behold a labyrinth of hydraulic pipes
Through which you'd play off wondrous waterwork;
Only, no water's left to feed their play.
Young, — you've a hope, an aim, a love: it's tossed
And crossed and lost: you struggle on, some spark
Shut in your heart against the puffs around,
Through cold and pain; these in due time subside,
Now then for age's triumph, the hoarded light
You mean to loose on the altered face of things, —
Up with it on the tripod! It's extinct.
Spend your life's remnant asking, which was best,
Light smothered up that never peeped forth once,
Or the cold cresset with full leave to shine?
Well, accept this too, — seek the fruit of it
Not in enjoyment, proved a dream on earth,
But knowledge, useful for a second chance,

Another life, — you've lost this world — you've gained
Its knowledge for the next. What knowledge, sir,
Except that you know nothing? Nay, you doubt
Whether 't were better have made you man or brute,
If aught be true, if good and evil clash.
No foul, no fair, no inside, no outside,
There's your world!

           Give it me! I slap it brisk
With harlequin's pasteboard sceptre: what's it now?
Changed like a rock-flat, rough with rusty weed,
At first wash-over o' the returning wave!
All the dry dead impracticable stuff
Starts into life and light again; this world
Pervaded by the influx from the next.
I cheat, and what's the happy consequence?
You find full justice straightway dealt you out,
Each want supplied, each ignorance set at ease,
Each folly fooled. No life-long labour now
As the price of worse than nothing! No mere film
Holding you chained in iron, as it seems,
Against the outstretch of your very arms
And legs i' the sunshine moralists forbid!
What would you have? Just speak and, there, you see!
You're supplemented, made a whole at last,
Bacon advises, Shakespeare writes you songs,
And Mary Queen of Scots embraces you.
Thus it goes on, not quite like life perhaps,
But so near, that the very difference piques,
Shows that e'en better than this best will be —
This passing entertainment in a hut
Whose bare walls take your taste since, one stage more,
And you arrive at the palace: all half real,
And you, to suit it, less than real beside,
In a dream, lethargic kind of death in life,
That helps the interchange of natures, flesh
Transfused by souls, and such souls! Oh, 't is choice!
And if at whiles the bubble, blown too thin,

Seem nigh on bursting, — if you nearly see
The real world through the false, — what *do* you see?
Is the old so ruined? You find you're in a flock
O' the youthful, earnest, passionate — genius, beauty,
Rank and wealth also, if you care for these:
And all depose their natural rights, hail you,
(That's me, sir) as their mate and yoke-fellow,
Participate in Sludgehood — nay, grow mine,
I veritably possess them — banish doubt,
And reticence and modesty alike!
Why, here's the Golden Age, old Paradise
Or new Eutopia! Here's true life indeed,
And the world well won now, mine for the first time!

And all this might be, may be, and with good help
Of a little lying shall be: so, Sludge lies!
Why, he's at worst your poet who sings how Greeks
That never were, in Troy which never was,
Did this or the other impossible great thing!
He's Lowell — it's a world (you smile applause),
Of his own invention — wondrous Longfellow,
Surprising Hawthorne! Sludge does more than they,
And acts the books they write: the more his praise!

But why do I mount to poets? Take plain prose —
Dealers in common sense, set these at work,
What can they do without their helpful lies?
Each states the law and fact and face o' the thing
Just as he'd have them, finds what he thinks fit,
Is blind to what missuits him, just records
What makes his case out, quite ignores the rest.
It's a History of the World, the Lizard Age,
The Early Indians, the Old Country War,
Jerome Napoleon, whatsoever you please,
All as the author wants it. Such a scribe
You pay and praise for putting life in stones,
Fire into fog, making the past your world.
There's plenty of 'How did you contrive to grasp

The thread which led you through this labyrinth?
How build such solid fabric out of air?
How on so slight foundation found this tale,
Biography, narrative?' or, in other words,
'How many lies did it require to make
The portly truth you here present us with?'
'Oh,' quoth the penman, purring at your praise,
"'T is fancy all; no particle of fact:
I was poor and threadbare when I wrote that book
"Bliss in the Golden City." I, at Thebes?
We writers paint out of our heads, you see!'
'— Ah, the more wonderful the gift in you,
The more creativeness and godlike craft!'
But I, do I present you with my piece,
It's 'What, Sludge? When my sainted mother spoke
The verses Lady Jane Grey last composed
About the rosy bower in the seventh heaven
Where she and Queen Elizabeth keep house, —
You made the raps? 'T was your invention that?
Cur, slave and devil!' — eight fingers and two thumbs
Stuck in my throat!

                    Well, if the marks seem gone
'T is because stiffish cock-tail, taken in time,
Is better for a bruise than arnica.
There, sir! I bear no malice: 't isn't in me.
I know I acted wrongly: still, I've tried
What I could say in my excuse, — to show
The devil's not all devil . . . I don't pretend,
He's angel, much less such a gentleman
As you, sir! And I've lost you, lost myself,
Lost all-l-l-l- . . .

                    No — are you in earnest, sir?
O yours, sir, is an angel's part! I know
What prejudice prompts, and what's the common course
Men take to soothe their ruffled self-conceit:
Only you rise superior to it all!

No, sir, it don't hurt much; it's speaking long
That makes me choke a little: the marks will go!
What? Twenty V-notes more, and outfit too,
And not a word to Greeley? One — one kiss
O' the hand that saves me! You'll not let me speak,
I well know, and I've lost the right, too true!
But I must say, sir, if She hears (she does)
Your sainted . . . Well, sir, — be it so! That's, I think,
My bed-room candle. Good-night! Bl-l-less you, sir.

Fears and Scruples

1876

I

Here's my case. Of old I used to love him
    This same unseen friend, before I knew:
Dream there was none like him, none above him, —
    Wake to hope and trust my dream was true.

II

Loved I not his letters full of beauty?
    Not his actions famous far and wide?
Absent, he would know I vowed him duty;
    Present, he would find me at his side.

III

Pleasant fancy! for I had but letters,
    Only knew of actions by hearsay:
He himself was busied with my betters;
    What of that? My turn must come some day.

IV

'Some day' proving — no day! Here's the puzzle.
    Passed and passed my turn is. Why complain?
He's so busied! If I could but muzzle
    People's foolish mouths that give me pain!

'Letters?' (hear them!) 'You a judge of writing?
  Ask the experts! — How they shake the head
O'er these characters, your friend's inditing —
  Call them forgery from A to Z!

'Actions? Where's your certain proof' (they bother)
  'He, of all you find so great and good,
He, he only, claims this, that, the other
  Action — claimed by men, a multitude?'

I can simply wish I might refute you,
  Wish my friend would, — by a word, a wink, —
Bid me stop that foolish mouth, — you brute you!
  He keeps absent, — why, I cannot think.

Never mind! Though foolishness may flout me,
  One thing's sure enough : 't is neither frost,
No, nor fire, shall freeze or burn from out me
  Thanks for truth — though falsehood, gained —
      though lost.

All my days, I'll go the softlier, sadlier,
  For that dream's sake! How forget the thrill
Through and through me as I thought 'The gladlier
  Lives my friend because I love him still!'

Ah, but there's a menace someone utters!
  'What and if your friend at home play tricks?
Peep at hide-and-seek behind the shutters?
  Mean your eyes should pierce through solid bricks?'

XI

'What and if he, frowning, wake you, dreamy?
  Lay on you the blame that bricks — conceal?
Say "*At least I saw who did not see me,*
  Does see now, and presently shall feel" ?'

XII

'Why, that makes your friend a monster !' say you:
  'Had his house no window? At first nod,
Would you not have hailed him?' Hush, I pray you !
  What if this friend happen to be — God?

A Forgiveness

1876

I am indeed the personage you know.
As for my wife, — what happened long ago, —
You have a right to question me, as I
Am bound to answer.

                    ('Son, a fit reply !'
The monk half spoke, half ground through his clenched
        teeth,
At the confession-grate I knelt beneath.)

Thus then all happened, Father ! Power and place
I had as still I have. I ran life's race,
With the whole world to see, as only strains
His strength some athlete whose prodigious gains
Of good appal him : happy to excess, —
Work freely done should balance happiness
Fully enjoyed ; and, since beneath my roof
Housed she who made home heaven, in heaven's behoof

I went forth every day, and all day long
Worked for the world. Look, how the labourer's song
Cheers him! Thus sang my soul, at each sharp throe
Of labouring flesh and blood — 'She loves me so!'

One day, perhaps such song so knit the nerve
That work grew play and vanished. 'I deserve
Haply my heaven an hour before the time!'
I laughed, as silvery the clockhouse-chime
Surprised me passing through the postern-gate
— Not the main entry where the menials wait
And wonder why the world's affairs allow
The master sudden leisure. That was how
I took the private garden-way for once.

Forth from the alcove, I saw start, ensconce
Himself behind the porphyry vase, a man.

My fancies in the natural order ran:
'A spy, — perhaps a foe in ambuscade, —
A thief, — more like, a sweetheart of some maid
Who pitched on the alcove for tryst perhaps.'
'Stand there!' I bid.

                          Whereat my man but wraps
His face the closelier with uplifted arm
Whereon the cloak lies, strikes in blind alarm
This and that pedestal as, — stretch and stoop, —
Now in, now out of sight, he thrids the group
Of statues, marble god and goddess ranged
Each side the pathway, till the gate's exchanged
For safety: one step thence, the street, you know!

Thus far I followed with my gaze. Then, slow,
Near on admiringly, I breathed again,
And — back to that last fancy of the train —
'A danger risked for hope of just a word

With — which of all my nest may be the bird
This poacher covets for her plumage, pray?
Carmen? Juana? Carmen seems too gay
For such adventure, while Juana's grave
— Would scorn the folly. I applaud the knave!
He had the eye, could single from my brood
His proper fledgeling!'

                 As I turned, there stood
In face of me, my wife stone-still stone-white.
Whether one bound had brought her, — at first sight
Of what she judged the encounter, sure to be
Next moment, of the venturous man and me, —
Brought her to clutch and keep me from my prey:
Whether impelled because her death no day
Could come so absolutely opportune
As now at joy's height, like a year in June
Stayed at the fall of its first ripened rose:
Or whether hungry for my hate — who knows? —
Eager to end an irksome lie, and taste
Our tingling true relation, hate embraced
By hate one naked moment: — anyhow
There stone-still stone-white stood my wife, but now
The woman who made heaven within my house.
Ay, she who faced me was my very spouse
As well as love — you are to recollect!

'Stay!' she said. 'Keep at least one soul unspecked
With crime, that's spotless hitherto — your own!
Kill me who court the blessing, who alone
Was, am, and shall be guilty, first to last!
The man lay helpless in the toils I cast
About him, helpless as the statue there
Against that strangling bell-flower's bondage: tear
Away and tread to dust the parasite,
But do the passive marble no despite!
I love him as I hate you. Kill me! Strike
At one blow both infinitudes alike

Out of existence — hate and love! Whence love?
That's safe inside my heart, nor will remove
For any searching of your steel, I think.
Whence hate? The secret lay on lip, at brink
Of speech, in one fierce tremble to escape,
At every form wherein your love took shape,
At each new provocation of your kiss.
Kill me!'

　　　　We went in.

　　　　　　　　　Next day after this,
I felt as if the speech might come. I spoke —
Easily, after all.

　　　　　　'The lifted cloak
Was screen sufficient: I concern myself
Hardly with laying hands on who for pelf —
Whate'er the ignoble kind — may prowl and brave
Cuffing and kicking proper to a knave
Detected by my household's vigilance.
Enough of such! As for my love-romance —
I, like our good Hidalgo, rub my eyes
And wake and wonder how the film could rise
Which changed for me a barber's basin straight
Into — Mambrino's helm? I hesitate
Nowise to say — God's sacramental cup!
Why should I blame the brass which, burnished up,
Will blaze, to all but me, as good as gold?
To me — a warning I was overbold
In judging metals. The Hidalgo waked
Only to die, if I remember, — staked
His life upon the basin's worth, and lost:
While I confess torpidity at most
In here and there a limb; but, lame and halt,
Still should I work on, still repair my fault
Ere I took rest in death, — no fear at all!
Now, work — no word before the curtain fall!'

The 'curtain'? That of death on life, I meant:
My 'word,' permissible in death's event,
Would be — truth, soul to soul; for, otherwise,
Day by day, three years long, there had to rise
And, night by night, to fall upon our stage —
Ours, doomed to public play by heritage —
Another curtain, when the world, perforce
Our critical assembly, in due course
Came and went, witnessing, gave praise or blame
To art-mimetic. It had spoiled the game
If, suffered to set foot behind our scene,
The world had witnessed how stage-king and queen,
Gallant and lady, but a minute since
Enarming each the other, would evince
No sign of recognition as they took
His way and her way to whatever nook
Waited them in the darkness either side
Of that bright stage where lately groom and bride
Had fired the audience to a frenzy-fit
Of sympathetic rapture — every whit
Earned as the curtain fell on her and me,
— Actors. Three whole years, nothing was to see
But calm and concord; where a speech was due
There came the speech: when smiles were wanted too
Smiles were as ready. In a place like mine,
Where foreign and domestic cares combine,
There's audience every day and all day long;
But finally the last of the whole throng
Who linger lets one see his back. For her —
Why, liberty and liking: I aver,
Liking and liberty! For me — I breathed,
Let my face rest from every wrinkle wreathed
Smile-like about the mouth, unlearned my task
Of personation till next day bade mask,
And quietly betook me from that world
To the real world, not pageant: there unfurled
In work, its wings, my soul, the fretted power.
Three years I worked, each minute of each hour

145

Not claimed by acting : — work I may dispense
With talk about, since work in evidence.

Perhaps in history ; who knows or cares?

After three years, this way, all unawares,
Our acting ended. She and I, at close
Of a loud night-feast, led, between two rows
Of bending male and female loyalty,
Our lord the king down staircase, while, held high
At arm's length did the twisted tapers' flare
Herald his passage from our palace, where
Such visiting left glory evermore.
Again the ascent in public, till at door
As we two stood by the saloon — now blank
And disencumbered of its guests — there sank
A whisper in my ear, so low and yet
So unmistakable !

          'I half forget
The chamber you repair to, and I want
Occasion for one short word — if you grant
That grace — within a certain room you called
Our "Study," for you wrote there while I scrawled
Some paper full of faces for my sport.
That room I can remember. Just one short
Word with you there, for the remembrance' sake !'

'Follow me thither !' I replied.

          We break
The gloom a little, as with guiding lamp
I lead the way, leave warmth and cheer, by damp
Blind disused serpentining ways afar
From where the habitable chambers are, —
Ascend, descend stairs tunnelled through the stone, —
Always in silence, — till I reach the lone
Chamber sepulchred for my very own

Out of the palace-quarry. When a boy,
Here was my fortress, stronghold from annoy,
Proof-positive of ownership; in youth
I garnered up my gleanings here — uncouth
But precious relics of vain hopes, vain fears;
Finally, this became in after years
My closet of entranchment to withstand
Invasion of the foe on every hand —
The multifarious herd in bower and hall,
State-room, — rooms whatsoe'er the style, which call
On masters to be mindful that, before
Men, they must look like men and something more.
Here, — when our lord the king's bestowment ceased
To deck me on the day that, golden-fleeced,
I touched ambition's height, — 't was here, released
From glory (always symbolled by a chain!)
No sooner was I privileged to gain
My secret domicile than glad I flung
That last toy on the table — gazed where hung
On hook my father's gift, the arquebuss —
And asked myself 'Shall I envisage thus
The new prize and the old prize, when I reach
Another year's experience? — own that each
Equalled advantage — sportsman's — statesman's tool?
That brought me down an eagle, this — a fool!'

Into which room on entry, I set down
The lamp, and turning saw whose rustled gown
Had told me my wife followed, pace for pace.
Each of us looked the other in the face.
She spoke. 'Since I could die now..'

                        (To explain
Why that first struck me, know — not once again
Since the adventure at the porphyry's edge
Three years before, which sundered like a wedge
Her soul from mine, — though daily, smile to smile,
We stood before the public, — all the while

Not once had I distinguished, in that face
I paid observance to, the faintest trace
Of feature more than requisite for eyes
To do their duty by and recognize:
So did I force mine to obey my will
And pry no further. There exists such skill, —
Those know who need it. What physician shrinks
From needful contact with a corpse? He drinks
No plague so long as thirst for knowledge — not
An idler impulse — prompts inquiry. What,
And will you disbelieve in power to bid
Our spirit back to bounds, as though we chid
A child from scrutiny that's just and right
In manhood? Sense, not soul, accomplished sight,
Reported daily she it was — not how
Nor why a change had come to cheek and brow.)

'Since I could die now of the truth concealed,
Yet dare not, must not die — so seems revealed
The Virgin's mind to me — for death means peace,
Wherein no lawful part have I, whose lease
Of life and punishment the truth avowed
May haply lengthen, — let me push the shroud
Away, that steals to muffle ere is just
My penance-fire in snow! I dare — I must
Live, by avowal of the truth — this truth —
I loved you! Thanks for the fresh serpent's tooth
That, by a prompt new pang more exquisite
Than all preceding torture, proves me right!
I loved you yet I lost you! May I go
Burn to the ashes, now my shame you know?'
I think there never was such — how express? —
Horror coquetting with voluptuousness,
As in those arms of Eastern workmanship —
Yataghan, kandjar, things that rend and rip,
Gash rough, slash smooth, help hate so many ways,
Yet ever keep a beauty that betrays

Love still at work with the artificer
Throughout his quaint devising. Why prefer,
Except for love's sake, that a blade should writhe
And bicker like a flame? — now play the scythe
As if some broad neck tempted, — now contract
And needle off into a fineness lacked
For just that puncture which the heart demands?
Then, such adornment! Wherefore need our hands
Enclose not ivory alone, nor gold
Roughened for use, but jewels? Nay, behold!
Fancy my favourite — which I seem to grasp
While I describe the luxury. No asp
Is diapered more delicate round throat
Than this below the handle! These denote
— These mazy lines meandering, to end
Only in flesh they open — what intend
They else but water-purlings — pale contrast
With the life-crimson where they blend at last?
And mark the handle's dim pellucid green,
Carved, the hard jadestone, as you pinch a bean,
Into a sort of parrot-bird! He pecks
A grape-bunch; his two eyes are ruby-specks
Pure from the mine: seen this way, — glassy blank,
But turn them, — lo the inmost fire, that shrank
From sparkling, sends a red dart right to aim!
Why did I choose such toys? Perhaps the game
Of peaceful men is warlike, just as men
War-wearied get amusement from that pen
And paper we grow sick of — statesfolk tired
Of merely (when such measures are required)
Dealing out doom to people by three words,
A signature and seal: we play with swords
Suggestive of quick process. That is how
I came to like the toys described you now,
Store of which glittered on the walls and strewed
The table, even, while my wife pursued
Her purpose to its ending. 'Now you know
This shame, my three years' torture, let me go,

149

Burn to the very ashes ! You — I lost,
Yet you — I loved !'

           The thing I pity most
In men is — action prompted by surprise
Of anger : men? nay, bulls — whose onset lies
At instance of the firework and the goad !
Once the foe prostrate, — trampling once bestowed, —
Prompt follows placability, regret,
Atonement Trust me, blood-warmth never yet
Betokened strong will ! As no leap of pulse
Pricked me, that first time, so did none convulse
My veins at this occasion for resolve.
Had that devolved which did not then devolve
Upon me, I had done — what now to do
Was quietly apparent.

            'Tell me who
The man was, crouching by the porphyry vase !'

'No, never ! All was folly in his case,
All guilt in mine. I tempted, he complied.'

'And yet you loved me?'

            'Loved you. Double-dyed
In folly and in guilt, I thought you gave
Your heart and soul away from me to slave
A statecraft. Since my right in you seemed lost,
I stung myself to teach you, to your cost,
What you rejected could be prized beyond
Life, heaven, by the first fool I threw a fond
Look on, a fatal word to.'

           'And you still
Love me? Do I conjecture well or ill?'

'Conjecture — well or ill ! I had three years
To spend in learning you.'

'We both are peers
In knowledge, therefore : since three years are spent
Ere thus much of yourself *I* learn — who went
Back to the house, that day, and brought my mind
To bear upon your action, uncombined
Motive from motive, till the dross, deprived
Of every purer particle, survived
At last in native simple hideousness,
Utter contemptibility, nor less
Nor more. Contemptibility — exempt
How could I, from its proper due — contempt?
I have too much despised you to divert
My life from its set course by help or hurt
Of your all-despicable life — perturb
The calm, I work in, by — men's mouths to curb,
Which at such news were clamorous enough —
Men's eyes to shut before my broidered stuff
With the huge hole there, my emblazoned wall
Blank where a scutcheon hung, — by, worse than all,
Each day's procession, my paraded life
Robbed and impoverished through the wanting wife
— Now that my life (which means — my work) was grown
Riches indeed ! Once, just this worth alone
Seemed work to have, that profit gained thereby
Of good and praise would — how rewardingly ! —
Fall at your feet, — a crown I hoped to cast
Before your love, my love should crown at last.
No love remaining to cast crown before,
My love stopped work now : but contempt the more
Impelled me task as ever head and hand,
Because the very fiends weave ropes of sand
Rather than taste pure hell in idleness.
Therefore I kept my memory down by stress
Of daily work I had no mind to stay
For the world's wonder at the wife away.
Oh, it was easy all of it, believe,
For I despised you ! But your words retrieve
Importantly the past. No hate assumed

151

The mask of love at any time ! There gloomed
A moment when love took hate's semblance, urged
By causes you declare ; but love's self purged
Away a fancied wrong I did both loves
— Yours and my own : by no hate's help, it proves,
Purgation was attempted. Then, you rise
High by how many a grade ! I did despise —
I do but hate you. Let hate's punishment
Replace contempt's ! First step to which ascent —
Write down your own words I re-utter you !
'*I loved my husband and I hated — who*
He was, I took up as my first chance, mere
Mud-ball to fling and make love foul with!' Here
Lies paper !'

     'Would my blood for ink suffice !'

'It may : this minion from a land of spice,
Silk, feather — every bird of jewelled breast —
This poignard's beauty, ne'er so lightly prest
Above your heart there ...'

      'Thus?'

        'It flows, I see.
Dip there the point and write !'

        'Dictate to me !
Nay, I remember.'

      And she wrote the words.
I read them. Then — 'Since love, in you, affords
Licence for hate, in me, to quench (I say)
Contempt — why, hate itself has passed away
In vengeance — foreign to contempt. Depart
Peacefully to that death which Eastern art
Imbued this weapon with, if tales be true !
Love will succeed to hate. I pardon you —
Dead in our chamber !'

True as truth the tale.
She died ere morning; then, I saw how pale
Her cheek was ere it wore day's paint-disguise,
And what a hollow darkened 'neath her eyes,
Now that I used my own. She sleeps, as erst
Beloved, in this your church: ay, yours!

                              Immersed
In thought so deeply, Father? Sad, perhaps?
For whose sake, hers or mine or his who wraps
— Still plain I seem to see! — about his head
The idle cloak, — about his heart (instead
Of cuirass) some fond hope he may elude
My vengeance in the cloister's solitude?
Hardly, I think! As little helped his brow
The cloak then, Father — as your grate helps now!

Halbert and Hob

Here is a thing that happened. Like wild beasts whelped, for den,
In a wild part of North England, there lived once two wild men
Inhabiting one homestead, neither a hovel nor hut,
Time out of mind their birthright: father and son, these — but —
Such a son, such a father! Most wildness by degrees
Softens away: yet, last of their line, the wildest and worst were
    these.

Criminals, then? Why, no: they did not murder and rob;
But, give them a word, they returned a blow — old Halbert as
    young Hob:
Harsh and fierce of word, rough and savage of deed,
Hated or feared the more — who knows? — the genuine wild-
    beast breed.

Thus were they found by the few sparse folk of the country-side;
But how fared each with other? E'en beasts couch, hide by hide,
In a growling, grudged agreement: so, father and son aye curled
The closelier up in their den because the last of their kind in the
    world.

Still, beast irks beast on occasion. One Christmas night of snow,
Came father and son to words — such words! more cruel because
    the blow
To crown each word was wanting, while taunt matched gibe, and
    curse
Competed with oath in wager, like pastime in hell, — nay, worse:
For pastime turned to earnest, as up there sprang at last
The son at the throat of the father, seized him and held him fast.

'Out of this house you go!' — (there followed a hideous oath) —
'This oven where now we bake, too hot to hold us both!
If there's snow outside, there's coolness: out with you, bide a spell
In the drift and save the sexton the charge of a parish shell!'

Now, the old trunk was tough, was solid as stump of oak
Untouched at the core by a thousand years: much less had its
    seventy broke
One whipcord nerve in the muscly mass from neck to shoulder-
    blade
Of the mountainous man, whereon his child's rash hand like a
    feather weighed.

Nevertheless at once did the mammoth shut his eyes,
Drop chin to breast, drop hands to sides, stand stiffened — arms
    and thighs
All of a piece — struck mute, much as a sentry stands,
Patient to take the enemy's fire: his captain so commands.

Whereat the son's wrath flew to fury at such sheer scorn
Of his puny strength by the giant eld thus acting the babe new-
    born:

And 'Neither will this turn serve!' yelled he. 'Out with you!
    Trundle, log!
If you cannot tramp and trudge like a man, try all-fours like a dog!'

Still the old man stood mute. So, logwise, — down to floor
Pulled from his fireside place, dragged on from hearth to door, —
Was he pushed, a very log, staircase along, until
A certain turn in the steps was reached, a yard from the house-door-
    sill.

Then the father opened eyes — each spark of their rage extinct, —
Temples, late black, dead-blanched, — right-hand with left-hand
    linked, —
He faced his son submissive; when slow the accents came,
They were strangely mild though his son's rash hand on his neck
    lay all the same.

'Hob, on just such a night of a Christmas long ago,
For such a cause, with such a gesture, did I drag — so —
My father down thus far: but, softening here, I heard
A voice in my heart, and stopped: you wait for an outer word.

'For your own sake, not mine, soften you too! Untrod
Leave this last step we reach, nor brave the finger of God!
I dared not pass its lifting: I did well. I nor blame
Nor praise you. I stopped here: and, Hob, do you the same!'

Straightway the son relaxed his hold of the father's throat.
They mounted, side by side, to the room again: no note
Took either of each, no sign made each to either: last
As first, in absolute silence, their Christmas-night they passed.

At dawn, the father sate on, dead, in the self-same place,
With an outburst blackening still the old bad fighting-face:
But the son crouched all a-tremble like any lamb new-yeaned.

When he went to the burial, someone's staff he borrowed —
    tottered and leaned.
But his lips were loose, not locked, — kept muttering, mumbling.
    'There !
At his cursing and swearing !' the youngsters cried : but the elders
    thought 'In prayer.'
A boy threw stones : he picked them up and stored them in his vest.

So tottered, muttered, mumbled he, till he died, perhaps found rest.
'Is there a reason in nature for these hard hearts?' O Lear,
That a reason out of nature must turn them soft, seems clear !

Never the Time and the Place

Never the time and the place
    And the loved one all together !
This path — how soft to pace !
    This May — what magic weather !
Where is the loved one's face?
In a dream that loved one's face meets mine,
    But the house is narrow, the place is bleak
Where, outside, rain and wind combine
    With a furtive ear, if I strive to speak,
    With a hostile eye at my flushing cheek,
With a malice that marks each word, each sign !
O enemy sly and serpentine,
    Uncoil thee from the waking man !
        Do I hold the Past
        Thus firm and fast
    Yet doubt if the Future hold I can?
This path so soft to pace shall lead
Thro' the magic of May to herself indeed !
Or narrow if needs the house must be,
Outside are the storms and strangers : we —
Oh, close, safe, warm sleep I and she,
    — I and she !

Bad Dreams, I

Last night I saw you in my sleep:
  And how your charm of face was changed!
I asked 'Some love, some faith you keep?'
  You answered 'Faith gone, love estranged.'

Whereat I woke — a twofold bliss:
  Waking was one, but next there came
This other: 'Though I felt, for this,
  My heart break, I loved on the same.'

Inapprehensiveness

We two stood simply friend-like side by side,
Viewing a twilight country far and wide,
Till she at length broke silence. 'How it towers
Yonder, the ruin o'er this vale of ours!
The West's faint flare behind it so relieves
Its rugged outline — sight perhaps deceives,
Or I could almost fancy that I see
A branch wave plain — belike some wind-sown tree
Chance-rooted where a missing turret was.
What would I give for the perspective glass
At home, to make out if 't is really so!
Has Ruskin noticed here at Asolo
That certain weed-growths on the ravaged wall
Seem' . . . something that I could not say at all,
My thought being rather — as absorbed she sent
Look onward after look from eyes distent
With longing to reach Heaven's gate left ajar —
'Oh, fancies that might be, oh, facts that are!
What of a wilding? By you stands, and may
So stand unnoticed till the Judgment Day,
One who, if once aware that your regard

Claimed what his heart holds, — woke, as from its sward
The flower, the dormant passion, so to speak —
Then what a rush of life would startling wreak
Revenge on your inapprehensive stare
While, from the ruin and the West's faint flare,
You let your eyes meet mine, touch what you term
Quietude — that's an universe in germ —
The dormant passion needing but a look
To burst into immense life !'
        'No, the book
Which noticed how the wall-growths wave' said she
'Was not by Ruskin.'
      I said 'Vernon Lee?'

Development

My Father was a scholar and knew Greek.
When I was five years old, I asked him once
'What do you read about?'
       'The siege of Troy.
What is a siege and what is Troy?'
          Whereat
He piled up chairs and tables for a town,
Set me a-top for Priam, called our cat
— Helen, enticed away from home (he said)
By wicked Paris, who couched somewhere close
Under the footstool, being cowardly,
But whom — since she was worth the pains, poor puss —
Towzer and Tray, — our dogs, the Atreidai, — sought
By taking Troy to get possession of
— Always when great Achilles ceased to sulk,
(My pony in the stable) — forth would prance
And put to flight Hector — our page-boy's self.
This taught me who was who and what was what:
So far I rightly understood the case
At five years old: a huge delight it proved

And still proves — thanks to that instructor sage
My Father, who knew better than turn straight
Learning's full flare on weak-eyed ignorance,
Or, worse yet, leave weak eyes to grow sand-blind,
Content with darkness and vacuity.

It happened, two or three years afterward,
That — I and playmates playing at Troy's Siege —
My Father came upon our make-believe.
'How would you like to read yourself the tale
Properly told, of which I gave you first
Merely such notion as a boy could bear?
Pope, now, would give you the precise account
Of what, some day, by dint of scholarship,
You'll hear — who knows? — from Homer's very mouth.
Learn Greek by all means, read the "Blind Old Man,
Sweetest of Singers" - *tuphlos* which means "blind,"
Hedistos which means "sweetest." Time enough!
Try, anyhow, to master him some day;
Until when, take what serves for substitute,
Read Pope, by all means!'
                                        So I ran through Pope,
Enjoyed the tale — what history so true?
Also attacked my Primer, duly drudged,
Grew fitter thus for what was promised next —
The very thing itself, the actual words,
When I could turn — say, Buttmann to account.

Time passed, I ripened somewhat: one fine day,
'Quite ready for the Iliad, nothing less?
There's Heine, where the big books block the shelf:
Don't skip a word, thumb well the Lexicon!'

I thumbed well and skipped nowise till I learned
Who was who, what was what, from Homer's tongue,
And there an end of learning. Had you asked
The all-accomplished scholar, twelve years old,
'Who was it wrote the Iliad?' — what a laugh!

'Why, Homer, all the world knows: of his life
Doubtless some facts exist: it's everywhere:
We have not settled, though, his place of birth:
He begged, for certain, and was blind beside:
Seven cities claimed him — Scio, with best right,
Thinks Byron. What he wrote? Those Hymns we have.
Then there's the "Battle of the Frogs and Mice,
That's all — unless they dig "Margites" up
(I'd like that) nothing more remains to know.'

Thus did youth spend a comfortable time;
Until — 'What's this the Germans say is fact
That Wolf found out first? It's unpleasant work
Their chop and change, unsettling one's belief:
All the same, while we live, we learn, that's sure.'
So, I bent brow o'er *Prolegomena*.
And, after Wolf, a dozen of his like
Proved there was never any Troy at all,
Neither Besiegers nor Besieged, — nay, worse, —
No actual Homer, no authentic text,
No warrant for the fiction I, as fact,
Had treasured in my heart and soul so long —
Ay, mark you! and as fact held still, still hold,
Spite of new knowledge, in my heart of hearts
And soul of souls, fact's essence freed and fixed
From accidental fancy's guardian sheath.
Assuredly thenceforward — thank my stars! —
However it got there, deprive who could —
Wring from the shrine my precious tenantry,
Helen, Ulysses, Hector and his Spouse,
Achilles and his Friend? — though Wolf — ah, Wolf!
Why must he needs come doubting, spoil a dream?

But then 'No dream's worth waking' — Browning says:
And here's the reason why I tell thus much.
I, now mature man, you anticipate,
May blame my Father justifiably
For letting me dream out my nonage thus,

And only by such slow and sure degrees
Permitting me to sift the grain from chaff,
Get truth and falsehood known and named as such.
Why did he ever let me dream at all,
Not bid me taste the story in its strength?
Suppose my childhood was scarce qualified
To rightly understand mythology,
Silence at least was in his power to keep:
I might have — somehow — correspondingly —
Well, who knows by what method, gained my gains,
Been taught, by forthrights not meanderings,
My aim should be to loathe, like Peleus' son,
A lie as Hell's Gate, love my wedded wife,
Like Hector, and so on with all the rest.
Could not I have excogitated this
Without believing such men really were?
That is — he might have put into my hand
The 'Ethics'? In translation, if you please,
Exact, no pretty lying that improves,
To suit the modern taste: no more, no less —
The 'Ethics': 'tis a treatise I find hard
To read aright now that my hair is grey,
And I can manage the original.
At five years old — how ill had fared its leaves!
Now, growing double o'er the Stagirite,
At least I soil no page with bread and milk,
Nor crumple, dogsear and deface — boys' way.

Epilogue

At midnight in the silence of the sleep-time,
   When you set your fancies free,
Will they pass to where — by death, fools think, imprisoned —
Low he lies who once so loved you, whom you loved so,
       — Pity me?

Oh to love so, be so loved, yet so mistaken!
   What had I on earth to do
With the slothful, with the mawkish, the unmanly?
Like the aimless, helpless, hopeless, did I drivel
      — Being — who?

One who never turned his back but marched breast forward,
   Never doubted clouds would break,
Never dreamed, though right were worsted, wrong would
    triumph,
Held we fall to rise, are baffled to fight better.
       Sleep to wake.

No, at noonday in the bustle of man's work-time
   Greet the unseen with a cheer!
Bid him forward, breast and back as either should be,
'Strive and thrive' cry 'Speed, — fight on, fare ever
       There as here!'

Index of Titles

Index of First Lines